WINTER IN TAOS

MABEL DODGE LUHAN (1879-1962)
TAOS, NEW MEXICO

i

SOUTH SIDE COMMUNITY HOUSE *(photograph by Ansel Adams)*

MABEL DODGE LUHAN

WINTER IN TAOS

Las Palomas de Taos/Taos, New Mexico
1996

WINTER IN TAOS reprinted from the original 1935 edition published by Harcourt, Brace, and Company, Inc., New York

FOREWORD copyrighted 1982 by Frank Waters

First Printing 1982

Second Printing 1987

Third Printing 1989

Fourth Printing 1996

ISBN 0-911695-50-8

Printed in the United States of America

Published by Las Palomas de Taos
P.O. Box 3400
Taos, New Mexico 87571
(505) 758-0975

Printing Production:
Horizon Communications
2710 San Diego, SE
Albuquerque, New Mexico 87106-3027
(505) 266-3431

Cover design by Janelle Harden

ILLUSTRATIONS

WINTER IN TAOS
Foreword
by
Frank Waters

Taos always has possessed the curious magic of seeming to be newly discovered by every person drawn into its mountain-ringed valley.

In earlier years, soon after the beginning of the century, its first painters heralded their discovery of a remote and virtually unknown locale to put on canvas. Gorgeous scenery and colorful people. Aspen groves turning butter-yellow against the spruce-blue mountain slopes, an adobe village with an aspect of Biblical times, Indians swathed in blankets, simple Spanish villagers tilling their fields. The artists were followed by early Anglo residents who found here a peaceful, slow tenor of life that far outweighed the lack of plumbing and other material comforts. Then came tourists to see its last vanishing aspects of "Old World Charm." Finally, the promoters of Progress who discovered an undeveloped area ripe for plucking. And now hordes of real estate agents, developers of commercial ventures of every kind; chain stores, galleries and souvenir shops galore, and huge condominiums mushrooming everywhere. :

One can conclude only that they all found here nothing in common; it varied with the individual. And one can venture that each discovered only an image of something he had brought within himself.

Mabel Dodge Luhan was a discoverer. One of the first, perhaps the best known and most influential in bringing others.

There's little need to recount here who she was, this wealthy socialite born of a conservative Buffalo banking family, whose colorful and controversial career spanned two continents. As a celebrated hostess at the Villa Curonia in Florence, Italy, in her salon at 23 Fifth Avenue in New York, and at Finney Farm at Croton-on-the-Hudson, she drew together the most famous characters of the time. Her foibles and idiosyncrasies, and her relationships with her first three husbands and a couple of lovers, were avidly publicized in the press, in critical biographical sketches, and by prevalent gossip. The public consensus was that she was willful, unpredictable, spoiled and selfish, a catalyst with the sole talent of attracting others.

But we don't need to rely on all these reports, most of which were written by persons who never knew her. Mabel has written the intimate details of her life in the four volumes of her **Intimate Memories** without sparing herself.

In the last volume, **Edge of Taos Desert**, she confesses to the desolation and emptiness of the life she had been living. The terrible sense of "non-being," of being "nobody in myself." The world she had known, our modern Euro-American civilization, was sterile, decadent, and dying. She and all others like her were not really living, but merely going through the motions. There grew in her the desperate need to break away, to start living at last.

How different this is from the picture of her as a social butterfly flitting heedlessly from one salon to another!

And then in the winter of 1916 she happened to come to Taos. Immediately her life changed. She divorced Maurice Sterne and married Tony Luhan, a blanketed Pueblo Indian. Together they built a seventeen-room adobe house on the edge of the Indian Reservation. To it, as to Villa Curonia and her Fifth Avenue salon, she

drew noted persons from everywhere. Through them Taos became world-famous.
How she and Tony ever managed to resolve their differences in race, language, and customs was a mystery. Every time Mabel went to New York for a visit, townspeople would assert, "This time she's going to get rid of that lazy, illiterate Indian." Mabel never did. They remained married for more than 40 years, until Mabel's death in 1962, followed by Tony's death five months later.

Just what did she discover in this backward adobe village of Taos that held her for the rest of her life?

Winter In Taos tells us. It doesn't rehash her tempestuous past life as revealed in her **Intimate Memories, Lorenzo in Taos,** several unpublished manuscripts, and her voluminous collections of papers turned over to the archives of Yale University. All this is behind her, as if forgotten. Instead, this short book, undivided into chapters, is one unbroken narrative of her new experience in simply living. Feelings, descriptions, and incidents merge into one another like the seasons. The daily activities in her own Big House, in the Pueblo, and the village. The details of planting, irrigating, and threshing oats and wheat. The ever-changing light on the Sacred Mountain. The rhythmic flights of her flock of pigeons, the characteristics of her cats, dogs, and horses. The beauty of flowers, the smell of sage after rain. Her trips through the valley with Tony . . . . What a sharp eye she had! And how warmly responsive she was to everything she saw.

Winter In Taos paints for us in fresh and flowing prose a living portrait of the valley as it was, that few of us remember today.

But it also presents a Mabel far different from the one whose reputation had obscured the woman beneath. A woman sensitive to her shortcomings, but who perversely always put her worst foot forward to public gaze. A woman known to her intimate friends as warm and thoughtful. Few people in town knew of the money, food, clothing, and personal help she constantly gave to those in need. As Claire Morrill reported, "Her reticence was somehow reserved for her virtues."

What Mabel discovered here, in short, was the simple life of the valley and herself, the essential, longed-for simplicity of just being. That they coincided is evident in these pages. For the first time her life came into clear focus.

It has been almost 50 years since this book was first published. The times have changed. The Taos she knew is gone. Mabel herself died 20 years ago. Most newcomers don't know who she was; many have never heard of her. But fortunately her Big House has not been bulldozed to make room for another huge modern condominium. It has been restored by **Las Palomas de Taos,** a non-profit educational organization which conducts classes in it for students and teachers in the art, culture, and history of the Southwest. Its preservation and utilization please me, for my memories of hours spent in it span more than 20 years of close friendship with Mabel and Tony. I think, too, its continued use would please both of them, whose very lives embodied the texture of their times.

This life is preserved for us in **Winter In Taos**, now reissued by **Las Palomas de Taos**. What a warm book it is, full of the juices of life. It brings back the freshness, the beauty of the valley before the Juggernaut rolled over it. And it also reminds us of the eternal verities of earth and sky that still remain untouched by time and change.

COURTYARD AND PIGEONS (*photograph by Ernest Knee*)

IN THE HILLS (*photograph by Edward Weston*)

ONE WINTER DAY, when Max came in to light the stove at eight o'clock, and all the smoke backed down into the room, and the sun shone through the blue cloud of it, and the air stayed just as it had been all night from the open windows—twenty above zero—I knew the soot had to be cleaned out of the chimney, the soot from the red flames of the pitch wood that makes the hottest fire of all as it burns, but hasn't the sweet smell of cedar and piñon, which turn into small, white ash after they are burned.

When I rang the buzzer for my coffee, Mrs. Gonzales brought it through the blue haze, looking east and west as she minced down the seven steps and across the room.

Her thoughts were easily read: "Inexplicable race! They keep the furnace going all night, but their windows wide open!"

I sat up in the thin, sunshiny, smoky air and dragged my mother's pink knitted shawl off the squat, carved bed post that Manuel made, and wrapped it around my shoulders.

"*Buenos días, Señora,*" murmured Mrs. Gonzales, "how are you today?"

"All right," I answered cheerfully, and suddenly emitted a loud sneeze, too unexpected and unprepared to reduce to a refined measure.

"*Dio!*" responded Mrs. Gonzales, looking at me rather cross-eyed through her drug-store specs.

"Nothing," I answered, sniffing backwards. "Max is going to clean the chimney this morning so you'd better give him some old newspapers."

The coffee seemed scalding hot in contrast to the atmosphere I drank it in, and I remembered how Kitty used to jump up on the bed on cold winter mornings like this, and her hot milk would be cool as soon as I poured it into the saucer and she didn't have to wait as usual, with her eyes half closed over the steam of it, pumping with her paws on the turquoise green blanket, impatient to sip, not daring to.

This Kitty still had then the glare of horror in her eyes that was in them when she followed Alexandra and me in the snow at the corner of the Kit Carson graveyard one evening. Lifting her paws and shaking them, crying with her face turned up to me, she had run back and forth across the frozen road, waving her tail in the air like a column of gray smoke. Seen only from the back, she looked gallant and gay and appeared to be dancing, but as soon as she turned around, one saw her anguished eyes were full of fear and hunger. How many evenings had she watched the sun go down and leave the world in its humming cold rigidity?

Then the sun was low and shining already below the branches of the cottonwood trees and turning the mountain into a big, crumpled rose. It is a lovely hour to walk about in the snowy lanes, hastening a little, for the bitterness of the night comes down fast. The air grows quiet. If there has been any wind, it ceases; and the snow squeaks under one's feet and the telegraph wires sing a low song. It is sweet, but it is bitter, too.

This gray Angora kitty knew that bitterness too well, apparently. Her white nose and shirt-front were dingy and neglected-looking, and she had a ring of solid lumps of matted fur around her neck. That night she just wouldn't go through it again, she seemed to be telling me, with her shrill, insistent meows. She raised her back and rubbed against my overshoes, swaying back and forth.

I picked her up and held her against my fur coat and she thrust her cold face inside my high collar and immediately began to purr.

I didn't know what to do with her. I didn't want a cat, although I must say I adore them. But a long time ago I made up my mind I had to choose between the joys of wild birds and our pigeons, and the pleasure of having two or three beautiful, long-haired pussies sitting around the big room on cushions, or washing their faces before the kitchen stove. There is nothing that makes a room so *interior*, so domestic and cozy and full of contentment as a nice cat beside the fire in the winter, or sitting in the open window in the summertime.

But they drive the birds away. Just when you are feeling the peace, perfect peace that emanates from a cat, it gets up, goes out into the garden, turns into a long, sinuous snake right in front of your eyes and starts to crawl up on some bird that you've begun to become acquainted with; and you have to start throwing stones or chasing it with a long stick; and all your participation in its smug enjoyment is turned into rage and indignation.

Really, to watch one's own dear cat slink out on a branch of the great cottonwood tree, wrap itself flat around it, and then try to dip the baby orioles out of their bag with a long paw shaped like a lemonade spoon, is just about enough to turn one on the whole race of them forever.

Our pigeons live in a Mexican village reared high up on thick, long posts. I love the expression of their frame houses, that have been added to by Jose for years. They lean strangely in all directions, and look like a settled community. We are always cutting back the branches of the big tree that grows so fast beside the stream, because the cats come at night from all around to steal the young squabs that can't fly yet. They cannot climb up the posts and reach them because the platforms of the houses jut out too far all around, but they climb the tree and drop onto the roofs from out of the branches. No matter what we do to protect the pigeons, the *placita* inside our wall is always strewn with gray and white feathers. One can hardly walk from the house to the gate any morning without that sudden pang in the heart that comes from seeing new feathers scattered on the grass or on the snow. Max sweeps them away, but more will be there.

It's bad enough to have the neighbors' cats always after our pigeons, but one doesn't know them personally; I couldn't bear it when our own nice kitties would be found sitting on their haunches in broad daylight, daintily pulling the feathers off a breast, mingling gray and white feathers with gray and white fur that seems of the same texture as well as color.

We didn't use to eat our pigeons ourselves because we felt we knew them so well. We just had them. For generations they have been born there in those lopsided residences, and they aren't afraid of anything because they don't have to be. After all, one or two marauding cats a night among three or four hundred pigeons is not enough to send a signal all the way through the community. In the daytime, sometimes a hawk flies over them, and then they all rise in one movement and circle round and round the big tree, the alfalfa field, the house; and Max sees them

7

alarmed and knows if it is an unusual time of the day for them to be circling about, or he notices if they seem nervous and their flight is troubled and broken, so he runs into the carpenter shop for his gun and shoots the hawk down; and pretty soon they're all sitting along the walls of the *placita* again, or walking up and down the portals in front of their *hacienda*.

All day long they are cooing and roucouling, and as their feathers resemble the cats' fur, so they seem to be purring like contented kittens. One has to pick one's way among them on the flagstones from the house to the gates. They feel they own the place and I guess they do. We never let cars drive in beside the portal any more as they used to do because the pigeons wouldn't move away fast enough and they were always being run over. Finally I put a sign on the gates and closed them. It said: "Please don't drive in. The pigeons don't like it." This seemed enormously funny to an art dealer from Chicago, and he plucked the sign off and took it with him. If he'd ever lived with pigeons he would have understood. Poor fellow! What, in Chicago, can give him the unfailing feeling of wonder and bliss the pigeons thrill one with year after year and several times a day when, at their regular hours they rise and fly low over the place in a calm, even circling and circling, when the indescribable soft rushing sound of myriad wing-feathers, swift and exultant, sweeps by, showing the lovely color of the underside of the stretched wings, veering and slanting like a sail against a blue morning sky, or a mauve evening sunset? What picture in any art-dealer's rooms can give one such an immediate joy as the flight of the pigeons when they take their happy exercise morning, noon and evening? It is the very quick and core of living. If it is delicious to participate with the cat in the deep within the penetrating domestic quietude of the somnolent interior, yet it is not so precious and uplifting as the tender, wakeful participation with the birds.

And not only the beloved blue and gray and white and leaf-brown pigeons—but at different times in the year the others who come and go and come again. In the summer the blue birds and wild canaries in the trees along the ditch; wind birds with reedy notes that nest under the beams of the portal; orange and black orioles swinging on the branches; and wrens. Down in the orchard there is a mocking bird that comes back every year, and we like him, though he has a rusty voice. Once there was a magpie without a mate, who followed wherever I went upon the place—from house to house, or into the vegetable garden. He just went along, sitting on any near-by tree, flipping his tail, a jolly, incomprehensible soul. They say here it is unlucky to see a magpie all alone, and we always look for the second one; but with this solitary clown, it didn't seem to matter.

When the leaves are flying in the autumn, they gather together, all the delicate ones, meeting in the big trees or down in the branches of the apples, when the air is cold enough to freeze the left-over fruit and wither it so it falls and slowly rots on the ground with a mild, melancholy odor. They meet, and then they go south to the Rio Grande and down to Santa Fe and beyond.

Their places are filled by the coarser birds with black, shiny feathers and loud, insensitive voices. Rooks and ravens and crows, landing in the pale yellow stubble of the fields, marching like armies to gather the left-over seeds, feeding for a while on their slower, later journey south. I like them, too. They are more stimulating and exciting than the others who left before them.

After wandering about the country roads for a couple of hours, watching them in their brisk affairs, one hears them from the couch in the corner of the Big Room. They make one conscious of the fall, the crisp air, new cider, and a detective story after tea in the fire-light.

"Caw-w-w, caw-w-w, caw-w-w!" they cry, high up above the house, flapping their black wings, flying in the face of a hundred blackbirds who chase them ahead. One hears them out there in the early twilight, and they are going miles, miles away over rivers and deserts, skimming the valleys and soaring over mountains.

It is good to lie flat and let the tiredness of walking flow out of one. Take up one of the "Mysteries" that come in batches twice a week from the Villagra Lending Library in Santa Fe, and sink in!

That is the perfect moment for the companionship of a cat. Glancing up from the book, you see her watching an empty place in the room, with round-eyed wonder. What do they see and we do not? Why do they never smile or laugh like dogs and horses? And what valuable forces do they emanate that are so palpable they affect the surroundings? Little repositories of secret power, reservoirs of the ultimate that overflow upon us and heighten our consciousness of home!

But I had chosen birds and I didn't want this long-haired kitten I was carrying along with me. I held her for a few moments and we went on our way down to the village, and Alexandra said:

"They say a cat is lucky if it comes to you like that."

"But I can't start *cats* again! I renounced them years ago!"

I put her down on a strip of the road where only the dry, frozen earth remained after a noonday thaw, and I walked away as fast as I could, with Alexandra hurrying to keep up with me; but that kitty was as fast as we were. She cantered along beside me, not miauling any more, but alert, with shining eyes. She felt she was a part of something now; an incorporated feeling, I suppose. She belonged. The cold didn't matter so much any more, for she sensed there was a saucer of milk and a warm fire just ahead of us. We laughed and let her come along, and thought foolishly that she'd get tired and leave us. But we didn't know that kitty yet.

When we came to Canyon Road leading into the village, and met automobiles hurrying to get home, or going to the post office for the evening mail, I had to pick her up again.

It was dark, now, the evening comes so quickly, as soon as the sun is down; and she was a gray blur, chasing along beside me in the snow.

"Oh, *Kitty!* I don't *want* you," I told her; but she paid no attention. She was a small, fierce, lone cat, and determined to belong.

"Don't you want a nice little cat?" I offered her to several people at the little, crowded post office. But no! Everybody who wanted a cat already had one.

So she came home. She never went out much in the cold after that night. Max put a nice box of earth in the sunny plant room and she understood it at once. She followed me all over the house and insisted upon sleeping on my bed under the yellow quilt. When Tito came near her she grew four inches taller and laid her ears back flat; she used to utter ferocious growls, transfixing him with glassy eyes that seemed to dominate him—but that was just his pretense. He would stand rigid, not moving anything but his eyes. He was a small, red and white imitation of a fox, only his tail curled right up over his back, and he had the domestic expression.

When Kitty tried to overcome his will, he would be motionless except for a kind of vibration running through him, and for the slow, sideways roll of his soft brown eyes when he would steal a look, now and then, to see how long she would hold it. They would stand, poised like that, for perceptible minutes, and he seemed to be staring into space; then suddenly he couldn't stand it another moment and he'd break it with a leap right at her that made her rise in the air like a puffball with explosive spittings coming out of it. Then they'd be off—up the stairs, down again, around and around, till she would pick a high spot and land upon it, glowering down at him for some time and complaining in a high, low, indignant growl:

"Well, really! I'm not going to put up with it! I've never been chased like that in my life!" Up and down from treble to bass, her crossness ranged. Yet all the time her little face looking just the same; not constructed to express anything but innocent wonder, and she couldn't look cross, no matter how she felt! Only the eyes held over a trace of horror from the past.

Tito joined our family one June. He arrived from nowhere, one day, and began sitting around the garden on his haunches at a little distance from where we all gather in the summertime, on the platform that bridges the Acequia Madre, under the swinging willow branches. He just sat here and there, observing. He wasn't very attractive, then. He skulked, he let his tail hang anyhow instead of curling it briskly up backwards, and his eyes were evasive.

"What on earth is *he* hanging around here for?" I exclaimed one afternoon at tea time. There were several of us there, Tony and Donnan and Garth and their father and mother. It was a lovely wide-open summer afternoon, with the sun trickling through the swaying willows and the brown water flowing beneath us.

"He just comes and *sits!*" Garth said.

"Got some reason, maybe," Tony answered, looking sage.

Sure enough. In a day or two, it was evident that Pooch had developed again that irresistible attractiveness that comes upon her every six months.

So we began to throw stones, not at, but in the direction of the little red fox, who let his tail drag more and more. But though he ran when we raised our arms, he only went in circles, reappearing shortly at the other end of the garden, or slinking up the steps out of the alfalfa field.

14

In the evening, he sat patiently on the doorstep. I deputized the twins to drive him away whenever they saw him in the daytime, and at night, when they left here to go over to their house. But Garth can't help liking all animals, and he said:

"That little red dog walks on his hind legs when you don't antagonize him."

He stayed for weeks like that, apparently unfed, and with nothing to encourage him. Certainly Pooch did not, for by reason of her considerable age, while she was interesting to others, she herself seemed to feel indifferent.

Finally—it was long after her seasonal fascination was over—I got used to seeing him there, always waiting politely at a short distance, sitting on his haunches, bright-eyed and delicate, and persistently hopeful. I stopped stamping my foot at him and crying, "Go away!" And once I suddenly *saw* him. I noticed the early morning sun shining through his red hair and making him incandescent; and he was like a little burning bush.

"Poor boy!" I said. "Come here," and I held my hand out to him.

He delicately picked up a little dry stick and, hanging his head, he walked slowly over and offered it to me with some embarrassment. Of course, from that moment *he* belonged! We fed him and named him Tito the Second, after Sally's adopted dog Tito.

It was no time at all before he raised his tail up and strutted about with a curve in his neck; and soon he felt he was the watchman here and responsible for our safety. He produced a high, shrill, indignant bark that he sounded an alarm with whenever a stranger entered our gate, and if one of the wandering horses and cows, that are turned loose in the winter, tried to come inside the garden at night, he almost lost his reason with excitement and rage. Not a day passed that he didn't give me a present: a leaf or a little stone, or a twig. Whenever I came in the gate, after being away from the house, he rushed out, with Pooch alongside, to meet me; and his ears pricked up and he always had a present in his mouth. If I were forgetful or unnoticing, he brushed against my feet and made small, soprano noises to call my attention back to him. Then I had to bend down and take it.

If he were shut outside too long on those cold days, he scratched very politely at the front door, and when I opened it, he came in sideways, deprecating and half-apologetic, but smiling and offering me a stone or a scrap of wood. Then I had to take it and say, "Thank you, sir," and hide it. He was pleased and satisfied and he flung himself down before the fire by the side of Pooch, who gave a groan, as much as to say, "Oh, my poor bones! How they ache! But thank the Lord we have this good fire!"

Tito was always exquisite and polite and perfectly clean

in the house. We often wondered where he came from, for he must have had a home and someone to teach him how to behave. He had a sweet loyalty and devotedness—what did he do with it before he joined us? I couldn't imagine him anywhere but here.

Even Tony couldn't place him, and didn't think he was either an Indian or a Mexican dog; he called him "Little Tramp" and never really seemed to accept him, because Tito didn't smile at him much, or bring him presents. He walked rather stiffly and warily on tiptoe around Tony, with his eyes turned sideways, glancing watchfully.

When my breakfast tray was ready, Tito knew, as if by magic, the exact moment it would reach me, and he managed to be outside the bedroom door that opens onto the garden steps. . . .

Pooch, of course, still accompanies this tray as it proceeds from the kitchen. This is the way it always happens: she has been let out of doors a half hour before, when Mrs. Gonzales opens the lavatory where she sleeps on two cushions beside a radiator, with the parrot cages poised above her on their long metal supports.

Dogs and parrots, geranium plants in the sunny windows, and Kitty's box—that is the place we wash our hands downstairs in this house, with the parrots jeering and laughing raucously at one's every move, or singing "taps" in sentimental saxophone voices. Sometimes one of them calls,

"*Perro! perro!* in such a convincing tone that the dogs come running, only to look foolish when they find nobody is there; and then, like as not, Polly will say, "*Parachito precioso!*" in a winsome tone of voice, and laugh and laugh. In the summer they stay out in the kitchen, and every morning all summer long Beatrice puts them outside the kitchen door with a dish of bath water under each of their cages, and they splash the water all over in the sunshine and flap their green wings and yell. They yell at every passer-by, at Indians on horseback, at the milkman, or the other delivery boys. They give loud, exultant shrieks, or jeers of laughter. Their laughter is so loud, up and down the scale, it can be heard all over the hill, sounding like two maniac women. Myron, up in his room, working on his typewriter, way down at the other end of the place, frowns and wonders why such things have to go on, and Andrew, inside his studio over across the fields, frowns and thinks a few exasperated thoughts, and finally, I, who am right overhead writing in my bed, jump up and call Beatrice from the window.

"Beatrice! Beatrice!"

"Ah ha-a-a-a-a! *Bueno!*" reply the two parrots loudly, cocking their heads up at me and ruffling their head feathers.

"Beatrice! Will you please remove those parrots!" I exclaim.

18

"I sure will, but what shall I do with them?" she answers. "Put them somewhere else!"

Presently I hear a little procession of two wending its way around back of the house and to the front. They carry the birds, who are giving cries of triumph. They love attention, any attention. This journey around the garden is delightful, they think. They duck up and down on their perches and open their beaks and let out the loudest blasts they can.

The girls carry them down to the Patio, which is as far away from me as they can go. The Patio is open on the west side with a little board walk across the front and two sides of it that has a roof supported on white wooden pillars. The fourth side is the wall of the log cabin. There are three or four dwarf fruit trees, sickle pears and apples, and tall hollyhocks, iris plants and delphinium flowers in this little enclosure, and it is a sweet place and very peaceful, until the parrots are deposited there.

When they see they are to be left alone, as the two girls turn away, giggling, they really put their hearts into their throats. They shout in loud, rapid chords of protest. "Wha! Wah! Wah-h-h," they both bawl hoarsely.

In my quiet room I only hear a faint, thin, faraway sound now. I don't mind it. But pretty soon the telephone rings:

"Beatrice! Do those parrots have to be left out there in that Patio?"

"Well, my God. I don't know what to do with them birds!"

They are brought back to the kitchen and she covers them up with two dark shawls.

"Is that nice?" asks Tony, coming in unexpectedly. "I think even parrots got to have some fun." And he carries them outside the back door again and sets them down in the sun.

Now Pooch steps out of the back hall door in the cold early morning, shivering and snuffling. She has never gotten over her ten cold winters in that garage. With a bleak expression, she trips a few steps, stops, sniffs, goes on a couple of steps, then crouches on bent knees in the snow, wholly feminine. She looks from one side to the other, her bat ears laid back against her head, her eyelids drooping and an expression of woe and disillusion upon her haggard, black countenance. She cannot believe life will ever be different from that instant when she has to pause there in the snow between the back door and the kitchen door.

Imagine this portly atom shivering out in that great early-morning landscape, with blue-shadowed snow stretching away to the hills two or three miles eastward where the sun has only just popped over the ridge.

On her stiff, thin legs she trips along; her stylish little

feet are cold now, so she tries to hurry as much as she can, swinging her sleek rear. When she comes to the place where, on the other side of the door it is all warm and odorous of bacon frying and hot toast and coffee, she stands and stares, with bulging eyes that stick out on the two sides of her round black head, her two threadbare ears cocked up like ventilators. She stands shivering in the snow and she stares straight ahead as though she would will the door to open. She can smell the bacon just beyond, and a long drop of saliva escapes her worn jaw and falls to the ground. Her upper lip is caught back of one of her two remaining tusks, and this gives her a sardonic grin. Her eyes are wide and brilliant and intense, now, and she wills and wills.

But nothing happens, so she is obliged to do something about it. She stamps one small, neat forefoot and ejaculates, "Hur-r-r-r-rumph!" This is all she has left in the way of a bark, and it sounds like a very old, husky frog. She doesn't like to use it often, being ashamed of it, after the resonant contralto she once had.

The door opens, she darts in between feet and skirts, thankful and happy, feeling a miraculous salvation fresh every day!

As soon as the tray proceeds out of the kitchen, she follows it. Not any other tray, just that one. She maneuvers her way through swinging doors at just the right angle, so as not to get caught in between, nor yet to enrage the one who carries the tray by brushing against her feet; she slides in between other doors that open and are closed; following, she mounts the stairs and struts, stiff-legged, through the first bedroom till she comes to seven steps that lead down, where she stands and smiles broadly, wiggling her crooked, flat, inconspicuous tail (which is slightly worn out and threadbare, too, like her ears and elbows and knees). Her face is calm and amiable, with no trace of suffering left upon it.

"Well, well!" she seems to be saying, "how are *you* today?" just like Mrs. Gonzales! She proceeds down the seven steps with seven stiff jerks, and walks across the slippery floor, raising her front feet rather high, with a prancing movement. She comes up to the bed and throws a glancing smile and a sniff.

This particular morning, when the stove smoked and I sneezed and Pooch walked over and turned her back hopefully to the stove, at that instant I was shaken with another enormous sneeze.

Now a sneeze means something here in the winter. It's not just a bit of dust, or pepper, or fuzz. It means A Cold. When someone says, in Taos, "I've caught COLD," it means more than in other places. It means aches all over one, a stiff neck, coughs and stuffiness. I don't believe that people in other places have these common or garden, old-fashioned colds any more, as one has here. The only thing to do is to stay in the house for two days and get over it or else have it lasting on and on for weeks and spoiling all one's fun.

"All right," I thought, "I'll just stay in and have it, and while I'm in the house I'll go deeper and deeper into myself and this place, and feel it as consciously as I can. I love it so much,—hardly knowing what it is I love. Now I will *know* it."

So I sent for Max to fix the chimney, and while he was working, I went into the next room where Tony slept, and waited there till I could return to my own bed.

He came slowly up from his breakfast in the warm kitchen. That's the nicest room in the house from eight until ten every morning. All the woodwork is painted blue and the walls are whitewashed; there is a long table in the center with a blue oilcloth on it, and a big blue stove burning cedar wood.

A long row of windows, facing east, lets in plenty of sunshine across the geraniums, and there is a breakfast table under the windows on the west side of the room. There is always a lovely smell of oranges and coffee, bacon and eggs and toast, out there at that hour, and men love to eat breakfast there, close to the Source, with the cheerful hum and bustle of cooking going on, the eggs still sizzling on the plate, the butter melting on the crisp toast.

All the men who have ever stayed with us, have liked their breakfast out in our kitchen, but women always like a tray in bed. I do myself. I like a perfectly silent breakfast, with plenty of hot coffee on a pretty tray with flowered napkins, rose-colored chickens on the dishes, and no one saying a word. Only the little animals coming and going and living their own lives and not talking to me out loud.

I could hear Tony thinking on the stairs as he came slowly up. He was almost thinking out loud, feeling what was in the air, reading the signs of the day in the atmosphere.

"Smoky?" he asked, raising up his nose when he came in.

"Max is cleaning out the chimney in my room," I told him. "My room didn't warm up, and I sneezed." I sniffed to show him. "So I'm going to stay in bed today."

"Too bad," he said, sympathetically. "You keep your room too icy-cold at night."

"Oh, I love it cold, so you feel as though you're breathing in thin ice; but I love it to get warm *quick* as soon as I wake up. But this morning my coffee got cold before I could drink it."

"You better look out," he said, warningly, "you going to catch a bad cold sometime."

"What are you going to do today?" I asked, changing the subject.

"I'm going over to Arroyo Seco and trade some oats for some beans," he told me.

Right away I saw the roomful of pale oats Tony harvested that fall. He planted several big fields of them on his land and I thought they would never be through hauling them in the truck in the long white sacks.

Our granary in the corral was half full of wheat, too, so we had to store the oats in the small end room at the cottage, where the maids sleep, at the end of the board walk across the alfalfa field. The oats filled the floor and reached up the walls, boarded off so the door could be opened: thirty thousand pounds of them, a big crop for this country. From springtime until autumn, how much work had gone to produce them!

The big field in Prado, two fields out towards the Pueblo, and the field across the ditch in front of Tony's house, had first to be plowed and harrowed, and then deeply irrigated.

How rich and welcoming the deep brown earth looked when it was ready to plant in May! The Prado field had had wheat in it last year and the stubble had been plowed under, and the others had had old alfalfa that was worn out and needed to be resown. One always plants a crop of oats in the field along with new alfalfa seed, for it can be harvested while the alfalfa plants are growing their roots during the first year. If one is lucky and wise, one gets a good stand of alfalfa at one sowing, but sometimes it's a failure and has to be sown once or twice more.

The fine seed is thrown on, and it settles on the dampened surface of the earthlike dust; it clings and breaks open and sends a little tentacle as fine as a hair down into the dark beneath. If all goes well, it develops into a tenacious root two or three feet deep in the ground, that gives three crops a season here, and four or five in lower altitudes. We always cut two of the crops, but leave the third for the horses to graze on, because it comes too late to mature and flower. The cold nights of September prevent that.

But sometimes the seed is blown away before it takes, by a fierce spring wind that sweeps everything before it, that is good to break open the sticky buds of the leaves on the trees, but deadly for the delicate surface of a newly-sown field. Or, if not wind, maybe a sudden rain comes down and washes the seed off the ground so that it will run away in rivulets and be lost in ditches.

Just a mild rain will float alfalfa seed away and let the oats stick there, sown in. A heavy down-pour, though, will unstick oats, and a cloudburst will uncover even corn seed that is planted beneath the surface—though that is a rare occurrence.

They tell a story about the hard luck of the Indians in one of the Pueblos below here on the Rio Grande, who

26

planted their crops of wheat and that went well; but later, when the time came to plant the corn, the ground dried up on it. You can't irrigate corn until it is well sprouted above ground, for it is too tender, so if there is too much wind and no mild rains, the seed withers. The Indians danced the Corn Dance to make it rain, but without success. They said, "Let's take the little Jesus into the fields and see if He will help them." So they carried Him from the church all across the cornfields and asked Him to make rain for them.

He did. That very night there was a cloudburst that washed out every bit of corn seed they had planted! They didn't think that was right, so they took the Virgin out across the ruined fields, and they bowed to her and said: "Now look at the mess your Son has made!"

We were lucky in our season. The little first-year alfalfa leaves, as small as three-leafed clover, showed below the tall stalks of oats on all the lands where they had been thrown.

Every once in a while, after the oats are up, you'll see Tony walking slowly around this near-by field after sundown, peering down, trying to see signs of the new alfalfa. When I see him doing that, I go over and join him, for it's a heavenly thing to walk about in the early June fields after the sun has set; the earth is still warm and the air is full of scent of flowers, and the wild birds are settling down after the sweet excitement they have been fluttering in all day, feeding the small new birds in the nests.

Tony says it never rains while the little birds are still unfledged. "That is taken care of by 'Someone'!"

So he was lucky in his crops and all those oats, that protected the slower growth, came up tall and green. Twice, three times they have to be irrigated during the summer, carefully, so as not to injure the little plants at their feet; the water to be guided across as evenly as possible with a hoe, not flooding it, nor yet allowing it to stand.

Not to overdo the irrigation, and yet to have plenty, is the problem, for too much water makes the stalks shoot up overhigh and all goes to foliage instead of condensing into grain. But farming is not all luck. Of all man's occupations, it is perhaps the most portentous, depending so much, as it does, upon two other things: knowledge and energy.

There is so much that must be *known*, and not only from the books, or the almanac and all the farmer's manuals, but from experience. From making mistakes and profiting by them, from trying things over and over again until just the right quantity, measure, weight and quality will bring the desired results. From studying the locality, the season, the prevailing habits of nature, from endless observation and care.

Then, the energy it takes! The everlasting fight against inertia, fatigue and the onslaught of indifference,—the day-by-day attention to detail, the everlasting physical effort, and the relentless continuity of character it requires, make of it the most disciplinary activity I know of, so that a failure, when it comes, strikes at the center of a man, giving him a feeling of uneasiness and inferiority and bad conscience; a discouragement with himself, and a sense of being without real power. And rightly so, for if a man has not too large a portion of land to take care of, if he has the proper horse or machine power in addition to his own strength, if he has studied and informed himself about his land's conditions, he can by his continuous effort force it to repay him and support him, so when his crops are successful, he has the greatest self-content. Unless accidental conditions of weather or drought defeat him, he has conquered nature and himself and feels a vast satisfaction that goes beyond the economic one.

> ("Let it please thee to keep in order a moderate-sized farm that so thy garners may be full of fruit in their season.")
>
> HESIOD.

In the autumn, when the field turns yellow, the farmer walks in it again in the early twilight and examines the heads of his oats to see if they are firm and meaty or just empty sheaths. He chews them to see if they are good fat kernels, or hairy and sterile.

All through the time when they are threshing, the Indians are chewing kernels of wheat and oats to test them; to find out their girth and solidity and whether they are rich and fat or shriveled and lean. As the threshing season goes along, the Indians bloom from the grain they have consumed, kernel or two at a time, through the days. They shine brighter, with mellower skins and more limpid eyes. They partake of the harvest, participating in the season's life, and one with it.

When I first came to this country, they threshed with horses that tramped around in a circle all day on the confined threshing ground. Afterwards they swept the wheat with brush brooms to remove the greater part of the chaff, and then the women cleaned it, little by little, standing upon a clean sheet and holding a basket overhead, letting the grain pour slowly downwards past their faces like a sheet of yellow rain. They knew the right time of day to do this, when a small wind would blow the dust and chaff off to one side and let the clean, fat grains heap up at their feet. But that was not all. Next it must be washed in the river, shaken in the basket and dried carefully.

There was only one, the first and only, threshing machine in the Pueblo then. The Indians harvested their crops by hand with scythe and sickle, threshed it with horses, and the women cleaned it. Then they ground it into coarse whole-wheat flour while the men and boys sang rhythmic grinding songs to them in the winter evenings.

CHARLEY AND ROSY (*photograph by Ernest Knee*)

RED RIVER CHURCH (*photograph by Edward Weston*)

When they had to bake, they ground it fresh in the measure they needed, and heating up the *adobe* ovens, shaped like breasts, outside each house, they had fresh bread that tasted like nuts. Wonderful bread.

Jo, who had lived away in Utah, came back and he contracted with the Government to buy a thresher; but many of the Indians turned away from it in distaste. Most of them felt instinctively that the old way was the best. The wheat passed through their hands, from the time they sowed it until it came back out of the earth to them and was baked into round, crisp loaves. It was flesh of their flesh.

One night someone set fire to the threshing machine—but, as ever, this active opposition worked to enforce its opposite, and another monster soon replaced it. Another and another. Now there is the Government machine, owned by the community, maybe two of them; and Tony owns an old one that sputters and stops and works intermittently. One hardly ever sees the horses threshing any more, and there are tractors plowing the fields with Indian boys driving them.

Only old, old men are sometimes seen bending over a sickle in the fields, and the grain has been ground in the flour mill down town for years. This fall, the Indians ordered a mill to be placed in the Pueblo,—they are paying for it themselves with their compensation money,—and they asked for a mill that will give them the whitest flour.

If one passes a plate of brown and white mixed breads at a table where Indians and white people are eating together, the white ones always choose the brown bread, and the Indians invariably take the white!

The wheat we had in our granary, Tony made with his own threshing machine. The wheat is brought together, belonging to different Indians, the sheaves stacked in big round mounds with the heads all turned towards the center to avoid bad weather; some near the Pueblo, outside the walls, others farther away, just according to the position of the fields, generally in family groups. Then the machines move from place to place and thresh in the various neighborhoods.

The Government threshing machine is run at the expense of the Indian whose wheat or oats are being threshed. He pays for the gas and oil, the Indian boy who runs the engine, and the helpers. Of course, the helpers are usually sons and brothers and cousins.

In the case of Tony's machine, it is different. He threshes for one sack of grain out of every ten, and he buys his own fuel.

Now that the old thing is so worn out, it is a painful process! Sometimes it starts all right in the morning and then suddenly stops. A band has broken, or some part gives out. Tony drives down to the plaza to see if any garage has the piece they need; they haven't, but they will go out and take a look and see if they can make it! Or they will telephone to Pueblo or Denver and have it here in two days.

The machine stands idle—Indian boys sit on the fence or in the great straw-pile and gossip. One of them putters on the engine. They all wear aviator's caps to keep the smoke and oil out of their heads, and shapeless overalls— and they are covered with grease, for they don't know how to cope with those materials yet.

Sometimes Tony comes back with the needed new part. It is incorporated into the ancient contraption, after a great deal of puttering and trying and suggestions from every-body around, for Indians do not handle machinery with a simple turn of the wrist, the way they dance or grind corn! It is something they are slowly adding to what they already know, a new adaptation they want to make. If we should turn to ceremonial dancing and ritual, or to making our own flour and baking our bread, we would be awk-ward, too, and probably covered with flour!

All at once the machine comes to life, the boys give tri-umphant whoops, they begin feeding the sheaves down the chute and into the gaping mouth of the juggernaut.

Out shoots the chaff from the long funnel and down streams the trickle of grain.

Boys shovel it into capacious white sacks that have

33

Tony's name painted on them so he will be sure to know them and not lose them or have them stolen. Every year, however, he has to buy new ones. They melt away.

At the end of a good day, there are eight or ten fat sacks leaning against each other, and they have to be loaded onto a wagon or a truck and hauled home.

What with the broken parts and the way they let the engine run, wasting gasoline and oil when they are waiting to fix some other little discrepancy, and the boys that have to be paid something, either in wheat or money, probably the wheat of Indian threshing machines is worth its weight in gold, as one used to say!

It is no cheaper, either, for those who run the Government machine, because they don't understand it, and it, too, is frequently out of order; and they haven't any idea how they waste fuel.

When they planted and harvested and ground their grains all by hand, there was no cost and no waste—all pure gain for the labor they put into it. But in those days they planted less and they lived off their corn and wheat, with wild vegetables and wild game. They worked so constantly in the fields that they burned up the starch that poisons sedentary people.

In the wintertime, when they were not out in the fields, they hunted in the snow and they had perpetual ritualistic errands up and down the Sacred Mountain.

34

That kind of life is changing very fast. They got so much more grain by the use of the machines that they began to trade it to the merchants in greater bulk than they were accustomed to do.

Formerly, they only needed a few things from the stores: coffee, sugar, salt, calicos and silks—not much more; but with the coming of machines they began to trade wheat and corn for canned foods.

In those years before 1929, one could see the influence of American money in the Pueblo. Several Indians opened curio shops out there and neglected to cultivate their fields. They let the earth lie fallow, and they began to make cheap little drums, bows and arrows, small, uninspired pots, and even oil paintings of the Pueblo, Indian horses, and men.

There were so many tourists and they spent so much money, the Indians thought all the Americans in the States were coming here and that they were all rich!

But that changed like all things change, and this year they planted a great many crops; besides, they have just received back some lost lands under the Pueblo Relief Act; and each Indian will have about fifteen new acres to cultivate. The curio shops were on the wane; another year will see them gone.

With all those oats he raised, Tony will feed his horses and mine. I have only two or three, Charley and Nelly, and a new one we named Tony. But Tony himself has an endless number of unbroken black colts whose mothers, Rosy and Baby and Poppy, add to their herd every year. They are perfectly useless, but quite good-looking, for he had a fine Colorado stallion, named Luis, from the San Luis Valley, and when he died of blood-poisoning got from barbed-wire one winter when we were in Mexico, I couldn't resist a shaggy black and white pinto fellow that someone brought to show us, and I bought him, and now he adds to the collection every year.

Tony calls them "the family" and, like the pigeons, just has them. He knows each one personally and walks among them, talking to them. In the winter they are strewn all over the desert in the sunny snow behind the house, nuzzling it to find the grasses and bits of feed underneath.

Sometimes I get efficient-minded, and irritable at the thought of them all, like so many useless and unpaying guests, but I have to remember that, after all, Tony raises tons and tons of alfalfa every year to feed them, and oats, too; and besides, he feeds my horses along with them and I shouldn't complain, for I didn't get a cut off my old alfalfa field. It was worn out several years ago, in fact.

This autumn I steeled myself and broke it up. I hated to, for it has not been plowed for sixteen years, and it had well-known paths across it to the Pink House and to the orchard and to the corral, beside the board walk across the middle of it. But although it was lovely to look at, all it raised was short turf and bunches of stiff brown grass, and it was silly to go on calling it the alfalfa field.

I borrowed the Government tractor from the principal of the school, and an Indian boy came riding down on it. For several days the place was hideous with the noise it made, though there were, as usual, frequent pauses of silence while Santiago stood bending over it!

It cut deep, deep into the old field and turned back juicy, steaming furrows, almost black they were so rich and good; and it has been a pleasure all winter to look at them and to walk between them on the board walk when one goes over to the stable, or to one of the little houses.

For a month this fall, Max and Jose drove the truck out to the Pueblo day after day to haul the wonderful manure one gets there. Tony said we would take it from his corral, and there seemed to be an endless supply.

They piled it in a high, long heap beside the cedar poles that fence in the corral—thirty feet long and seven or eight feet high it was—pure feed for the exhausted land.

Now, whenever they have time between their other chores, they hitch up the wagon and drag it out and throw it over the naked furrows and onto the vegetable garden that lies between the field and the Pink House. To enrich old, unplowed earth, before planting a new crop of alfalfa, one has to spread a ton and a half of manure to the acre— and that's a lot of manure!

Besides feeding the oats, Tony trades them for corn or dried peas and beans. We have to feed corn to the pigs who have a sty beside the corral. They are fine red animals and the hog we had was the largest hog I ever saw. The way we got him was that some time ago, the Indian Agent gave the Pueblo Governor a sow for a present, because he wanted to improve the Indian stock, and the sow was about to have a litter. Well, the Governor told Tony if he would take her and feed her and the young ones until they were old enough to look after themselves, he would give him one of them. So Tony took her and she had twelve or some such vast number, and the Governor gave Tony one of the boys—and this was he!

One July afternoon I came back up the hill from a drive with Adrian, and Mary came out the garden gate to meet me. Her beautiful face was no more surprised than usual, in spite of her strange words. She announced:

"Mrs. Jeffers is going around in there with a gun in her hand, and she says there is a wild boar loose on the place!"

I couldn't get over the ground fast enough! I simply couldn't imagine what had happened. I hurried, ran, stumbled over the flagstones, dodging in and out of the high hollyhocks, and, as ever in the altitude, it was like wading in some dense invisible sand. I heard Adrian panting behind me, trying to keep up.

When we got to the front door there she was! Sure

enough, with a gun in her hand, a blue automatic, and a look of doom on her dear Irish face.

"What is it?" I gasped.

Her face was white as chalk. "That pig over in the corral got out and has gored three of the horses. . . ."

The two boys had seen it first. They were walking past the corral and heard the rumpus inside and when they looked they saw all the mares were driven into a corner and Charley was standing in front of them, defending them. The boar, infuriated, charged him again and again, and there were horrible red streaks on his white legs and chest. Blood and foam were dripping off the long tusks of the boar and he raged up and down, trying to get past the horse and reach the trembling mares. A little colt, confused by the uproar, dodged out past Baby, its mother, and was almost ripped by the lightning speed of the clumsy beast, but Baby shoved out past Charley and edged in front of her young one, and the boar struck, an upward slash of the powerful head that opened her belly, so the long, linked entrails hung down.

The boys ran and fetched their father, and Jose, coming back from cutting alfalfa, arrived. They all went into the corral with pitchforks to try and drive the boar back into his own pen, and it was then that Una got her gun, ready to shoot the animal if it turned on her men.

By the time I reached the house, it was all over, with

Rosy and Baby bleeding to death, and Charley covered with wounds. Blood, they told me, stood in pools all over the corral and there seemed little hope of saving the poor animals. Someone went for the doctor, not a vet, for we have none here, but a real doctor, and he came and sewed and sewed until all the gaping wounds were closed. As usual, I couldn't go near the place. I sat and shook in the Big Room while it was going on, and Robin sat behind me smoking his pipe. His voice was matter-of-fact and cool in telling about it, and this calmed me down.

"Charley was wonderful," he said, "the way he tried to protect his mares."

Adrian came in with his movie camera in his hand and his face white. He had been photographing the whole thing to show his friends in Hollywood, for they would not believe him when he told them about it, he said, unless he showed them the picture. "That doctor is shaking like a leaf," he said.

"But why?" I cried, "why did it happen? I didn't even know we had a wild boar!"

"Why, you know that old pig that is always lying down, sleeping, over there? He's the one. Jose says he took the sow away yesterday and put her in a separate pen because she was going to have a litter and the male might eat them, and this made him mad and he broke down his fence and started to attack the mares in his rage. Jose says he'd have killed them all if Charley hadn't been there!"

Oh, Charley! I could see him with his forefeet planted and his neck arched like a horse on a Greek frieze.

One summer afternoon's fury, and three months of daily care to remedy it, bathings and powdering with antiseptics, endless leading up and down to prevent stiffness and bound muscles and the loss for riding.

Tony had been away in Oklahoma when it happened, and when he came I told him: "Your big pig nearly killed the horses," and I described what had happened.

"I going to shoot him now," he answered, and did so.

The reason we keep pigs at all is to take care of the garbage from this house and any of the little houses that I lend or rent to friends. Every morning Jose comes to our back door with a pail and takes it away to the pigs, who instantly make way with it.

Only pigs will *not* eat orange peels, and there are always so many of those in the pen!

The pigeons eat dried peas or crushed corn or wheat. We feed them a little twice a day, and they have to hunt for the rest.

Of course beans we eat ourselves quite often, with *chili con carne*, one of the best meals in the world.

Tony is always giving his family a sack of beans or peas. They know how to make all kinds of good soups from them; and as he has seemingly endless nephews with their wives and nieces with their husbands—and now their children rapidly growing into large grand-nephews and nieces —there is always someone looking wistful.

Tony likes to help them and cheer them, for he is naturally patriarchal and born to be a head of a family. It is a pity he has no sons of his own; but he never did have any, though Molly said she heard that *all* these nephews are really his sons! A most interesting thought to outsiders, I presume.

That morning, when Tony came upstairs, he sat down in the red rocking chair beside the bed. He looked serene and ample and strong as a dike. When Frieda and Lorenzo first came and we were driving them up to Santa Fe from the train, Frieda, I remember, looked wonderingly at his broad back in front of her and exclaimed:

"Don't you feel he is like a *rock* for you to lean on?"

And I said, "No," uncertainly. But we had only been together five years then. Now, twelve years later, he seems like a rock; more than that, a mountain, that will support all the weight I can put on him. Nothing can really hurt a woman who has a man like this, to give her moral and emotional support. We could lose our houses and our horses, our friends, our health and our strength, but as long as we are together, we are immune from essential loss.

"I'm going to stay in bed all day and maybe do some work," I told him.

"Goin' to be a very cold day, seems," he answered, looking over to the snowy hills he could see from the window. "There go those snowbirds." He pointed his finger and I raised up so I could see down close to the ground outside, a whirr and a flick of tiny gray wings flitting by, cheeping; such small birds and so swift in the sunshine.

"Means more snow comin', maybe this evening."

"You coming home for dinner?"

"No, I guess I eat over there. You know I don't like to eat all alone. But better you stay in bed today and keep yourself warm."

He got up and raised his blanket over his shoulders and stood there looking massive, like Pharaoh, as Lorenzo always said. Then he leaned down and brushed his lips gently over my cheek.

"Look out!" I exclaimed crossly. "If I have a cold you'll catch it," and I pulled away from him.

He looked faintly critical, as he always does at any graceless gesture that anyone makes, though he said nothing about it, for he keeps his opinions to himself; but his dignity increased slightly and his gravity went deeper.

"Well, you know how easy it is to get a cold from someone," I explained, mollifying, and laughing a little.

"I think your heart take care of that if you let him," he

43

said, reproving. "Your heart, he stronger than cold or bad things like that, if you got a good heart. And my heart good."

"Oh, sure! I know it. But I can't forget all those things I've been taught! *You* know . . . !"

"White people know too much and feel too little," he answered. "Well, I goin'."

"Come here!" I cried, and stretched out to reach his hand and draw him down and give him a big kiss, for I felt the warmth he always knew how to release, flooding my nature and making my own heart good.

But there was just a shadow of reserve in his touch now; a check. We both ignored it. We were used to each other's ways and sure, at bottom, even though our nerves and muscles still sometimes revolted at dissimilar attitudes of mind and custom. It seems as though we make a new adjustment every day!

Mrs. Gonzales came clicking up the stairs on her high heels, and entered deprecatingly:

"*Con permiso*," she murmured, "Matilda says the sheep is all gone."

"Oh, dear!" I cried to Tony, "you'll have to do something about *that*, now."

In a corner between the wall of the kitchen and the wall of the back gate, we have a small cold chamber with a heavy wire door. As soon as the freezing winter is here,

44

we buy a steer and a sheep or a lamb, and have them butchered and hung on big iron hooks in there. Every morning Max brings the cook the cuts she wants for the day, and the meat has a wonderful taste. I don't like packing-house meat any more since I have grown used to Taos lambs and calves and steers and things.

It is a good feeling in the wintertime to know we are all stocked with provisions, so that even if we should get snowed in, as we were once, years ago, for thirteen days (though that was before the Highway was built), we have enough to keep us, right on our own place.

In the root-cellar, we have a heap of potatoes that Tony raised at his ranch at Tienditas; very sweet and fine they are, better than Colorado potatoes, though not very large, because they don't grow much after the real cold weather sets in up there in those high fields in the hills southeast of this valley.

And, besides potatoes, we have pumpkins and squash that he raised in the small field at Placita, and from our own vegetable garden here, we have carrots, beets, onions, cabbages and turnips, cucumbers, cantaloup and watermelons!

From our apple trees, we keep enough apples to last us through till the next crop, so we're forever having apple pies and puddings! We always have too many apples, so we can give away some to Max and Jose, and to Tony's family; and it is the same with the potatoes.

Then, in the storeroom, are the rows of glass pickles! Green tomato pickle, cucumber pickle, and piccalilli that were put up in the summer when the garden was over-flowing.

I like to think that we put up all our preserves: apple-butter, pears, peaches, apricots and plums; that we make our jellies of currants and quince, and apple flavored with mint; and our orange marmalade, too, and pear chips, that condiment flavored with ginger roots.

Something left over in me from my grandmother has made me turn back to these earlier ways of living, made me to enjoy my storerooms full of the fruit of the earth, though it has meant so much hard work to stock these dark cellars and these storeroom shelves, and has, prob-ably, cost more to fill them than to buy the efficient products of the shops. But as I don't like the shallow delights of delicatessens, where one buys half a pound of wonderful potato salad in a little paper boat, along with a dill pickle and two doughnuts, no more do I like the flaw-less preserved fruits of chain stores. They seem tasteless and without any background.

Food, one's own, home-grown food, reaches back into one's land, comes up along one's days through the seasons until it stands waiting on the storeroom shelves, or cool in the dark cellar. It seems more real, and more rich and full of wonder, when it comes before one on the table, than anything one can buy.

When I am sitting there eating, I can remember late summer days when the apples were just beginning to redden, and we walked in the orchard and pinched them on the trees; or the day when Tony so carefully put the pumpkin seed in the little trench he dug, which so soon sent up the strong shoots and grew and grew until all the ground was covered with great, twisting vines and huge umbrella leaves which hid the swelling orange globes; and here on the table is a grand pumpkin pie with whipped cream resting on it—and it came from nothing, nothing but that small flat seed. Isn't that wonder enough when one stops to think of it? I sit and eat and wonder.

Perhaps that's why I am so rude at my meals, and so often criticized for my silence and abstraction. Really, I am always thinking about my food when I eat it!

Strange, various, changing directions of human nature! While I turn away from those mass productions and the cans and jars of store goods, the Indians eagerly spend their few dollars or trade their grains for these, and forsake the fields and the wild vegetables that grow upon the southern mountain slope!

While I seek out a house in the Pueblo where the whole-wheat is still ground by hand, buy a small sack of it and take it home to Beatrice, who will bake it into the heavy, tan-colored loaves of nutty bread, the Indians are buying the light-weight loaves of bluish-white bread wrapped in oiled envelopes, bread that has no taste and no virtue, that has had the live germ in the wheat seed mechanically removed so the loaf will last indefinitely in the market and not start *living* on the counter!

The Indians are, by some kind of predilection, and by the destiny that has been determined for them by the influence of the Indian Bureau Schools, headed for Progress, a mechanical civilization and an undermined racial stock, while some of us white people are said to be regressing to an earlier mode of life instead of conforming to our present-day environment.

So be it! I stand by the true whole-wheat bread! And I will continue to take comfort in the thought of our stores of good food.

"Well," said Tony, "I stop by Mares' and see if he got any more them fatted sheep."

"See if he can butcher it and bring it by tomorrow, will you?"

He asked, "People comin'?"

"Yes. You know John and Claire and Pat will be here—and there'll be others right along."

"All right. I'll do my best. Then I'll go over to Arroyo Seco with my oats."

Calm and measured his tread down the little stairway where he had to keep his head bent all the way, so as not to bump it.

Max had been making rattles and shakings of tin in my room, and now he was finished. When I opened my door, I felt the lovely warm radiation from the stove, and smelled the faint perfume of the room coming out in the heated air. The sun was streaming in the eastern windows over the big table, and falling on the blond, glossy floor and its pale, hand-woven rugs.

This room was all in a light key, with walls whitewashed with a pale gray earth, and a low ceiling supported by four thick, twisted columns that Manuel carved out of big pine trees and painted white. The tables were in natural wood color, waxed, and so was the big, low bed that was built right there in the room, with its bedposts made of chunky, twisted pieces left over from the columns.

In the daytime, there was a marvelous, fine, hand-woven wool bedspread over it that I got in Mexico, embroidered in many colors of wool, with fantastic figures of animals and trees and fruits; but at night there was an eiderdown, covered with jade-green silk.

The bed stood beside a wide casement window that opened upon a long-reaching view. The Sacred Mountain faced right down upon it, beaming across field after field of Indian land, pale yellow stubble showing through the snow; and horses were meandering around, their dark, furry outlines looking as though they had been brushed in with Chinese ink on absorbent paper.

I hastened back to my place in the good bed and sighed with contentment. Nothing to do for a whole day—not to have to cope! I am able to cope, and one has to in this country; but I get tired of it, sometimes. I am not a born coper, like Evangeline; I have had to learn to do it. I have learned, but it is not my pleasure.

"My pleasure is in being very still and sensing things," I thought, as I experienced the exquisite relaxation of giving up.

"Still and all, if one hadn't *done* a lot of things and been through all the movements of life, one wouldn't have this fund of experience to draw on, or be able to sense all the many experienced pleasures and delights and pains and worries, too, that are suggested by the sights from my window, by the things about me in the room, by the odors and memories and associations that are the essences of activity and that, like poetry, are now the emotions of activity remembered in tranquillity."

I thought, "But for the coping and the managing, and all the crowding movements of life, the eternal adjustments and the never-ending 'fixing' one has to do in the house and garden, as well as in oneself, to keep order and harmony, cleanliness and beauty of some kind, but for all this often tiresome detail of life, one's soul would not be a storehouse; it is so true that the external life creates the inner, that is, if one really lives in each passing moment and takes into oneself its meaning and significance.

From my casement window, framed in silk curtains, jade green on one side and pale lemon yellow on the other, I saw Poppy out in the snowy field with her new little foal alongside her. They gleamed a burnished copper color in the sunshine, and beyond them the willows along the winding Acequia Madre were a deep, soft, Siennese red.

All the way to the mountain the willows burn softly through the winter, and the name of the Indian village is The Red Willow Pueblo. The tall cottonwood trees rise over the willows in a long, curving line, like gray smoke, and sometimes the line is interrupted by bunchy mountain elders with trunks branching from the roots like a knot of strong, gray serpents thrusting themselves upward.

The cottonwoods are tall trees, but the Sacred Mountain that rises like a dark wall of snow behind all that I see from my window, towers so high that it dwarfs them and makes them seem like a fragile, drifting vapor; and the horses look like tiny ants in comparison with it.

The two peaks of the mountain are white, where it leans against the blue sky, and it is shaped like a bow across the top; and in its deep recesses there is a perpetual coming and going all through the hours and all through the seasons. The Indians give life to it, and it gives life to them.

In the wintertime, one only knows the mountain from a distance, and then one can get it whole. One can pounder its vast bulk, and watch its changing forms and speculate upon the mysteries it hides within its canyons and in its deep folds. In the other months, one loses the mountain in the nearness of the mossy banks along its streams where the large mauve columbines grow and, looking up through green branches, one finds the sky is hidden by the leaves.

Early in the morning the mountain looks crumpled and as though a lot of pyramids were stacked against each other to form it, for the sun rises on its east and outlines its planes with deep blue shadow.

There is a canyon running diagonally up across it that seems to lead into its center, into the interior of the earth; a canyon with a fast-flowing stream coming down into the plain—and it, too, is edged with feathery cottonwood trees. From my window I can see the broad band of shadow cast by the rising wall of this canyon as it leaps up on the side of the main great mass of the mountain. Huge buttresses of rock zigzag down on the opposite side of the stream. It must be dark in there, now, where the water flows cold and still, although the sun shines golden on the outer slopes.

All along the base of this dark, snow-speckled giant, there is a light blue haze lying at this hour. These are the break-

52

fast fires, and smoke is curling out of a hundred chimneys up there in the Pueblo.

Like a flock, a tribe is actuated with a single impulse, where the simple, major needs are concerned. With no clocks to rule them, and no bells, save the school bell calling the children, and once in a while the church bell, yet they all move as one in a large rhythm of life in the winter: getting up, eating, caring for the horses and cows, going out and coming in, eating again, and going to rest.

From the top of one or the other of the two pyramidal piles of dwelling houses, the Governor or the War Chief calls his orders, and the voice reaches into every corner of the Pueblo. People talk and children laugh and play, uninterruptedly, but the voice penetrates consciousness and is noted and obeyed. The voice is the same, year after year, though the man changes. It is the same in tone and inflection, and it has the same inherited authority. It is the voice of the community.

Sometimes, on clear, still days, the sound of it comes down to our house, three miles away, just as, when the wind is right, the sound of the Pueblo church-bells reaches us.

The sounds we hear around our house, both near and faraway sounds, are pleasant to our ears. They are not so many or so complex that we cannot recognize them, every one. The dogs, talking among themselves, or barking when some stranger comes along, the horses whinnying in the fields, and the birds in their seasons, make the constant accompaniment of our days. Sometimes the sharp trot of a horse's hooves is heard passing behind the house, when someone is riding down from the Pueblo, singing, or a creaking wagon is passing slowly by, driven by a Mexican, selling wood.

The cars of the tradesmen come at their stated hours and bumble and buzz up to the kitchen door. First the milkman in a touring car at eight o'clock in the morning, and later on the little grocery truck from town, or the freighter from Ute Park bringing express boxes, or the telephone man to fix a loose wire. There are not many, and one grows to recognize them all, as well as the sound of our own two Fords, Tony's and mine, backing out of the garage, or coming up our hill.

Tony's engine was cold this morning when he left for Arroyo Seco, and he raced the engine to warm it up.

"Mother, you mustn't race the engine like that," John once said. "You run the heat through the cold steel and that ruins it." "I must remember to tell Tony that," I thought. We neither of us know beans about machinery.

Sometimes noises come across the alfalfa field from the corral: pigs grunting, or a sudden angry shriek out of one of the horses kept inside the stockade, who has been nipped on the flank by another. The mares are kept inside when the foals are only a few days or weeks old, and sometimes Charley, my white horse, is kept loose in there, too. The Pinto is always in the small corral behind the stables and granary. He is lonely and pokes his nose through the cedar posts and sometimes he reaches a hind leg and, wrinkling back his upper lip, gives a quick bite for the pure need of company and contact. Then, from inside the house, we hear hooves cracking on stout wood, and the high, angry whinny cutting the air; then Jose's voice shouting at them while the turkeys gobble with excitement.

All winter long we hear the sound of the ax; and outside my east window the woodpile is standing in cords. Eight feet long and four feet high and four feet wide, a cord costs five dollars, in green piñon, and we burn many cords throughout the winter, for we keep fireplaces going and stoves, too, as well as the coal furnace. The green wood is heavy with sap, and whenever he has a spare hour, Jose is out there chopping it up. We mix the dry wood with the green, for the fires burn longer so.

The ax comes down on a green log with a heavy, dead thump, quite different from the sharp, ringing split of steel on dry timber; the blade sticks in the sullen wood and squeaks when Jose works it back and forth to loosen it. The aroma of green piñon comes up and creeps into my room—delicious and aromatic.

Farther along towards the kitchen, Jose chops cedar for

the cooking stove. Cedar wood sparks out into the room and burns little spots on the floors and *serapes*, if one uses it in the open fireplaces, so we only have it for the closed stoves. It makes the best fire of all, and the blue smoke of it, rising fast and transparent out of the kitchen chimney that I see from my bed, has the smell of incense. No wonder it is a sacred tree to the Indians, for its fire is the purest and most intense of any wood, its odor is a subtle, soul-stirring perfume, and it never rots in the ground. A cedar fence post lasts forever.

Early in the morning, at any time of the year, one wakens to the faint sound of the ax coming to one from here and there in the valley. These distant rhythmical sounds accompany the dawn, and they give one a mild living thrill as one lies listening. Men in their homes cutting firewood before the sun is over the hill, while the birds are only just beginning to chirp and cheep, sleepily, convey a sense of life, and a good life, too.

From all over the valley, cocks crow in the early morning, and that is a happy sound, a homey sound that gives a sense of security and leisure. There is nothing like a cock-crow to ease the haste and hurry that people grow accustomed to in cities; it seems to say there is all the time in the world, take it easy, take it deep and take it easy!

Another winter sound we always have, is the red-winged woodpecker, knock-knock-knocking, pecking *adobe* out around window frames, forever making holes in houses, tapping on wood, busy, annoying bird that he is! But, oh! how lovely as he streaks across the blue sky, showing the bright red underwings! So rapid and skimming in his flight that the country people call him "Flicker."

He makes such human sounds, he often fools people. Once when Ward and Clyde were living in the Two Story House, they came in after dining out and they found a note pinned on the door that their little maid Marguerite had left for them. It said: "Be careful when you go upstairs. I heard someone up there and he hasn't come down!" It was the energetic Flicker, knocking on the roof, of course!

Often the sound of bells floats across the valley. Every morning at half-past six, Father rouses the village with the church bell that his Mexican rings; again at seven it peals out or comes faint and sad, according to the wind. And once more at seven-thirty.

He has the bell rung at noon and at five o'clock, so we all live, really, by Father's time. But there is another time, that of the railroad! It is apt to differ considerably from Father's, but usually we don't know that, for to get the "real" time, one has to call up the drug store, which has had it from Taos Junction, thirty miles away. Father's time has always been good enough for most of us.

Of course, people who come up from Santa Fe have still another time! We ask them for luncheon at half-past twelve, and they may arrive at one o'clock, and if one looks cold, they show their watches and say, "Well, it's half-past twelve by Santa Fe time," as though that were the only time in the world!

Once in a while the bell tolls and tolls, when someone has died, and before we had the Fire Siren at the Power House, if a building caught on fire, Father would have it rung fast, with agitated summoning strokes, so everyone would rush to the village to help put out the fire.

Sometimes the bell in the *morada* behind our house calls the Penitentes to a *Velario*. This is a smaller bell than the one in the Catholic Church in the village; it has a silvery treble, very high and clear.

Underneath me, in the dining-room, there is the click of the waxer that is being pushed across the black and red tiled floor; my bedroom is at the busy end of this long house, and I hear too much of that kind of thing!

I hear the dogs barking around the kitchen door whenever anyone comes, and I hear the stove-lids being clapped onto the stove, and I hear the telephone ring and the girls answering it. These are not agreeable sounds, they are the penalty for a room at this end of the house that looks northward to the Sacred Mountain.

The other end of the house is as still as a church! Starting at the lively kitchen, one can walk straight through ten rooms, each one growing more silent, but each one, alas! farther away from the view! Their windows open eastward on the desert behind the house, and they do look out upon a lovely line of hills. Their west windows open upon the columned portal that leads out on the *placita*, paved with flagstones, with the Acequia Madre curving around, and the big cottonwood tree throwing its shade over all.

The *placita* is like an outdoor room; there is a round flower-bed in the center of it which is only a black mound of manure, now, that each new snowstorm moistens and soaks until the rich liquor runs down to the roots of the plants asleep below. There are flower-beds outside the log cabin, where it juts out to balance the rainbow room at the other end of the portal, nearest the front door. Along and above the *acequia*, there is a wide border where all kinds of things are hidden in the earth, showing only scrawny, tangled branches, now, and the long, bare waving fingers of four weeping willow trees that hang over the platform across the stream, where we sit on summer afternoons.

This is a lovely place, of course. The big flags have hollyhocks and burning bushes thrusting up between them in July; the pigeons strut up and down and carry on their perpetual courtships; but it is an enclosed place. The cottonwood trees, the mountain elders and the willows shut in the *placita* and the house. One only catches glimpses through their branches of the little houses across the alfalfa field. The western horizon far away that we used to see so plainly when we first lived here, is hidden, now, by our own trees, and the trees that Manby planted forty years ago. The Sacred Mountain is hidden, too, by silver beech trees along the ditch outside the kitchen door.

I have to have a window that opens upon the mountain, and from my room, nothing stands between me and that open view of its sometimes calm, and sometimes stormy face.

The fantastic house that has grown slowly, room by room, stretches and sprawls out beneath me. First there was a long, coffin-shaped, bare box of a place containing the four original rooms that I bought when I came eighteen years ago. Jose's father lived in them and offered to sell when Tony approached him about it.

Tony always loved this piece of rising ground above the town on the edge of the Indian land. When he was a little boy, he came down here with his father, who knew how to do carpenter work, and he held the nails when his father cut a hole in the thick *adobe* wall and fitted a new window into one of the rooms for Jose's father.

This same window is in Tony's room, now; it is the room where his guns and hunting knives are locked in the carved

FROM MY WINDOW (*photograph by Ernest Knee*)

OUR SOUTH VIEW (*photograph by Edward Weston*)

guncase Manuel made for his Christmas present two years ago, and where all his Indian things are. In this room he has many confabulations with Indians who come to talk over things, sitting before the corner fireplace. On the chimney place there are some things people have given him, a bronze horse, a bronze deer, and a golden buffalo!

The old beamed ceiling is painted sky-blue and the walls are whitewashed. There are white muslin curtains on the long window that looks eastward over the desert, but on Tony's father's tall, narrow window, there is none, so one can see out onto the portal through the small, uneven panes.

There is a bed beside this window, where sometimes one of the nephews or a visiting Indian friend sleeps. It has a red and white patchwork quilt on it, made of little pieces of old-fashioned calico.

On the wall over the bed, there is a crucifix carved out of ivory, that Clarence gave Tony, and upon it hangs a small rusty rosary he found in the ground here on the place. There are some Indian paintings hanging on the walls; also a fishing basket, a coiled-up hair rope, a pair of beaded moccasins and some other Indian things.

The long, narrow window his father set in the wall looks out upon the portal that stretches from the front door to John's jutting log cabin. It is a little crooked, and its wooden frame, ten or twelve inches wide, is somewhat warped, but he would not have it changed and neither would I.

Once, a long while ago, my mother and Monty came to visit us here. Instantly I grew aware of the shortcomings of this house, the cooking, and all the lacks we had grown accustomed to; using oil lamps and open fires had become a matter of course.

It was autumn, and the sumptuous beauty had faded away from everything outside. I saw it all from their viewpoint, my patchwork of a house, and my rickety stables and corral that was picturesque enough to be a suitable background for the Holy Family, with its horses and sheep and pigs dawdling against the pale, weathered wood; but with my family here, it suddenly appeared run-down, inefficient and, in contrast with their own spick and span farm at Youngstown, it was, I realized, quite reprehensible.

Instead of being a large, comfortable, homey home for our familiar beasts, where sunrise and sunset beautified the old cedar posts and ancient sheds, and the animals dwelt in peace in their own quiet rhythm, it was revealed as a slipshod, careless, ramshackle affair, an eyesore, a deficit, a failure. Monty only knew model farms. Ours was not a model for anything but a painter or a Southwestern farmer.

And how I have loved it, this house built on different levels, a room or two at a time. The gatherings of all my past life are deposited here. Besides the regular furniture and pictures and books that came from Italy and France and New York, letters, in packets, that date all the way back to Buffalo, are stuffed into cabinets and drawers, and all kinds of curious odds and ends that have followed me down the years are tucked away in corners and shelves. Bits of china, silk, scraps of carving, parts of Buddhas, lacquer, incense, parchment and tooled leather throw out odd scents when one opens a cupboard door, or opens the heavy lid of some chest.

In the linen room, upon the top shelves, there are piles of remnants filled with the sweet smell of cedar with which the place is lined. Handwoven bits from Asolo, old curtains from the Villa Curonia, pieces of French embroidered dresses, long lengths of faded chiffon and muslin, batiste and mull. Presents of Indian beadwork, oddments of basketry and deerskin, Renaissance velvet, ecclesiastical gold fringe, are side by side with my Grandmother Ganson's patchwork quilt, made of squares of taffeta cut out of her old dresses. Fragrant little empty bottles from Chanel, Houbigant and Guerlain are hoarded there, too attractive to throw away, as are lovely little gilded and colored boxes of all shapes, kept to mail things in.

Every drawer in the house, when opened, throws out a curious odor and a rattle of some kind, for heads of Dresden shepherdesses or hands of *papier-mâché* angels from Italy

63

are to be found tucked away till the time comes to mend them, along with bits of gold or walnut carving, and rosettes, whorls or moldings that belong on the mirrors and chests and chairs and need to be replaced, but never are.

Then the piles of papers! Besides the letters of a lifetime, in many languages, there are all kinds of documents. Passports; bills of sale for horses, cars and cows; pamphlets written by friends; photographs waiting to be pasted in the big books; press clippings; old magazines with articles written either by myself or by someone I know; pictures of people; Indian paintings; Senate bills; picture puzzles; games; birth-certificates; manuscripts; canceled cheques; and tax receipts.

Paper! Paper! Paper! And how I hate paper. One of the things that sets all my nerves jangling, is to handle paper. Yet I am always having to hunt for a piece of it, always looking for a paper; and, strangely enough, there is a kind of order in the mass, so it can be found—or, if I fail, Spud succeeds in tracking it down.

So the house is a kind of treasure trove, but it is treasure that needs a key, and I am the only one who has it. No one else could possibly understand the origin and use of all the mingled fragments hidden away in it, and I can never catch up with it all or get it really assembled. When one is my age, and has never had the heart to throw away a pretty box or an interesting letter, or get around to having all the breakages of journeys and the daily wear and tear on delicate antiques repaired, it may be imagined what accumulation gathers about one.

Old colored glass stoppers from English bottles; strings of beads from everywhere under the sun; silk parasols and brocade bags stuffed into carved chests along with pieces of old Portuguese printed cotton, batiks from Bali, embroideries from Czecho-Slovakia, left behind by Reed and Maurice. Keepsakes of every kind from all kinds of people, stuffed away into dark corners. One couldn't have all the stuff out gathering dust. One thing edges another out of place, symbols in layers of thought, feeling, living, that has been and has passed away.

That is what the Big House is made up of. It is my home, it holds me, works me to death, bores me and will not let me go! The trees we planted have almost buried it, now; they tower in a great, green wall between us and the town. When I first came to live here in two or three rooms with Tony, we could look down the road and see all the way to the turn at the corner, and I said to him, then:

"I bet I'm going to spend all the rest of my life looking down that road!" I looked down along it for years, watching for him to come home, but now it is hidden. Nothing can be seen of it, not even the lights of an approaching car in the summertime, so thick are the leaves of the cottonwoods and elder trees along the "mother ditch" that curves along in front of the house below the flagstones that pave the courtyard.

The house grew slowly and it stretches on and on. At one end it piles up, for over the Big Room there is the bedroom where Tony sleeps, next to my room, and a big sleeping porch off of it; and from this room one climbs a steep little stairway up into a kind of lookout room, made of helioglass set in wooden columns on all four sides, where one has the views of all the valley, down to the village and beyond it to the horizon, up to the Pueblo and the Sacred Mountain, north to Frieda's ranch on the side of Lobo Mountain, and the Colorado mountains beyond it.

There is nothing on this bare, blue-painted floor but some *serapes*, and up here under the sky, winter and summer, one can lie in the sunshine and bathe in it until "untied are the knots in the heart," for there is nothing like the sun for smoothing out all difficulties.

On a lightning-conducting rod, a gold cock is reared high up from one corner of the roof of this sunroom, and it can be seen sparkling all the way to the Pueblo as it turns in the wind. Sometimes, when Tony and I are riding high up in the hills behind the house, we look down to find the long *adobe* building has melted into the earth and we cannot find it until suddenly the sun strikes the gold cock and it flashes a sign to us, showing where we live; and Tony says it reminds him of when he was young. He was staying with some Kiowa Indians in Oklahoma and the man he was visiting had twin daughters. They were beautiful, with smooth faces and long braids of shining hair that fell to the bottom of their skirts.

He liked them very much, he says, and they liked him. He stayed there all summer, and when he left, their father gave him a horse and saddle.

Early one morning he rode away home and the two girls stood and watched him go, waving their hands, and the country was so flat that he could look back and see them for a long, long time; even after he had gone so far that he couldn't see them any more, they still waited and they sent him flashes from a hand mirror, as was the way, over in that country.

"Finally I came to a place where I turned west away from there, and I looked back and they sent me a flash and that was the last one."

It is so good to ride horseback in the snow when the sun is high and warm. We used to take all the dogs, Pooch coming last, her ears back until the tips touch, and her eyes bulging; Tito ran like a rabbit among the sagebushes, leaping every once in a while; and Thyla, the Great Dane, and her big daughter, Donska, gliding with long strides in and out of cedar trees and piñons, looking so much like mountain lions that I was always afraid they would be shot by Indian boys out hunting, but now we don't have to worry.

No matter how cold it is, the snow is always melted under each sagebush, from the heat in its oil. The piñons and cedars have little icicles hanging from their tips, and we eat them as we go along, and chew the delicious pine needles. The snow crunches under the horses' hooves, and it is bright and sparkling and makes one's eyes ache; but in the shadows, it is a vivid blue.

Here in the hills, the snow is marked with many little patterns of the wild animals, and Tony has taught me to know them all, and which way they are going. Bobcat, coyote, jack rabbit and cottontail—they all come and go and cross each other.

The mare I ride this year, Nelly, has a little foal three months old. We have put a halter on him made of maguey fiber, with magenta and green tassels, and we take him along when we go out. He runs along ahead of us and turns back to meet us like one of the dogs. He loves these excursions, and he sniffs at every new trail he has never yet been on in this life, and he nozzles the snow and eats it and shakes his head and kicks up his heels. His large, tender eyes are shaded by thick, black lashes, and since he arrived in cool weather, he came well covered in a long, soft, fuzzy coat. We call him Chatto, and he knows this name, already, and comes when we call him or when we whistle.

From far away, down in the valley, we can hear a motor racing, or the high-school bell, or sometimes a rooster crowing out of the usual hours; we can see the smoke curling up from cozy houses and it is pleasant to warm one's heart by these signs—but sometimes when we are out riding, the snow begins to fall, softly. The sun goes and all the color. There is no wind and the big flakes come down in a leisurely way, turning over and over. Then there are no sounds to be heard except those very near us. We can hear our horses still crunching in the snow, and the dogs breathing, though we cannot see them a few feet away, for a snowfall shuts out the familiar sounds of life.

Yet, if one listens, there is something else one can hear in the silence, something very different from the homely noises of the distant village. Another world is opened up to one in the cessation and the stillness, another music that is hidden deep within the world, that is usually inaudible and that is impossible to describe.

We come home slowly, and our voices are muted. We dare not press our horses faster, for they cannot see the pitfalls they must avoid, the prairie dog holes and the loose stones. The dogs fall behind us, quietly, now, tails down; the little foal, Chatto, rubs against his mother's side, the snow gathering in his long lashes and thickening in his bushy mane. For his mane is bushy like the hair of the Indian boys before they have reached the year of initiation: soft and coarse and wild all at once. Later, it will fall over his neck in a long, smooth curve, like the Indian boys' hair when they return from their absence, with their heads sleek and the long, straight part running from the neck to the brow.

We have to follow the trail home through the snow that has covered it; we move through the bushes and trees that are suddenly white and bent under the swift and silent pressure, and we leave it to the horses to find the way. We reach our house before we expect it; it looms up all of a sudden, and if it is late afternoon, there will be a lighted window shining yellow.

When we shake off the snow and go in the house, there is a warm smell of the narcissus and hyacinths that bloom all winter there, and of freesia and jonquils in vases, lovely in the firelight, with hot tea and cinnamon toast.

But not more lovely than the cold, odorless world of ice and snow, where the piñon, cedar and sage are pungent with the magical oils they draw from the deep, living earth.

When I heard Tony's car start with a roar and then settle into a steady hum, and finally disappear down the hill to town, and I was left alone in my big, pale, quiet room, I pulled my books and magazines around me and began to turn over pages.

For thirty years I've been meaning to read Boswell's "Life of Johnson." Today I would really start it, but just at the moment I had that little drop in my heart that I always have when Tony leaves, even for a few hours. There is a certain fall in the emotional temperature of the place, at least for me, in his absences. The house is less alive, and things look less significant when he is gone. But he says the same thing happens when I am not there. So it must be all in our imaginations. But where he was, I thought, speeding along the road to Arroyo Seco, everything looked more vivid and real than this place where I was left alone.

I looked out of the window beside my bed and I could see all the way over to where he was going, by following the base of the Sacred Mountain, and the Lucero Creek, bordered by cottonwoods, that was along the base of the next one to it, the mountain that is just a huge spur of rock, like a tooth jutting into the clouds; and then Seco Mountain beyond.

I could not see the road he traveled, for it was lower along the valley. The Indian pasture and farmlands were between it and the foot of the mountains, and it was obscured for me by trees in the daytime, although I knew that if it were night and he was returning this way, I could see his car lights shining intermittently in and out all along the way back.

The air was so still and clear, today, that I recognized the Ford as it turned the corner down town and passed up Pueblo road, passed Dr. Martin's and on out along until it came to the two graveyards, across the road from each other, where it slowed down to turn north to Seco.

We have the prettiest graveyards in the world here in this valley, I believe: all sown with pale blue or white wooden crosses, where the wreaths of pink and red and orange paper roses hang since All Souls' Day, and have been wetted by snow and blanched by the sun, until they are mellowed and melted into a dream-like, impressionistic picture of their first hard, crisp contours. There is a small, rakish, turquoise blue cross planted out there with the letters "M.D." painted on it, that Bobby used to swear marks my grave; reflecting, I suppose, the belief of that time that I was buried here!

I could not hear the little car after it turned, but I knew well enough how it ran along between the meadows that are so green and swampy in the summertime, one always sees cows munching in there, buried up to their bellies.

The fields are blond with snow and pale, shining yellow grasses, now; and the sky above them is a cold, light blue, different from the burning depths of the black-blue of summer. They sweep, in a gentle rise, across to the foot of the range, and the Indian horses are dotted about on them. In the distance, little Indian *adobe* summer houses sleep like forgotten rectangular boxes, with a bare tree or two hanging over each of them. The winter landscape is vast and pale with blue shadows lying upon it, and the tender, smoldering red of the willow clumps beside the stream.

In a couple of moments, Tony reaches Placita, which is a cluster of houses alongside the Pueblo Creek. Here is a bridge it passes under, on its meandering way to Ranchito and Corierra and Cordóba, all small neighborhoods that once had, each, their own little water mills where they ground the wheat between round millstones. Now the wheels that carried the water are still, and the millstones are scattered over the valley. They are set up as curiosities, into sun dials, or used as stepping stones at gates. Two of them stand on edge at each side of the big gates of Gerson's Dairy, further along the road; several of them are inlaid between the flagstones of our courtyard; and two of these ancient Taos stones lean against Jeffer's tower in Carmel.

Spud's house stands just beyond and to the right of the bridge. The creek curves around his yard, and big trees border it. There is a hammock swung there in the summertime; and in the center of his place, between the little house and the little river, there is a sunken pool, lined with stones, with flax and iris blooming around it. The water runs close to the surface under these houses, and he only had to dig two or three feet to reach it.

He can open a gate and go through his Mexican neighbor's place and reach Miriam's alfalfa field; and her *adobe* house lies there near the Indian boundary, blond and pale like herself. There are several old apple trees in the front of it, and their trunks and branches shine red in the winter sunlight. There is a hammock hanging between two of them, but it is gray and rotted now, for Miriam went away for the winter and forgot to put it inside the house.

Behind Spud's house stands the house of a Mexican neighbor, and a small, beautiful chapel with a white painted, carved door. A tree-bordered road turns off the highway here and leads in over a cattle guard to a dear little cream-colored house that stands in a brown field, and whose windows and doors are bordered with pink. Big gray trees hang over it, and make a shelter, and it looks like a cottage in a fairy tale. It is an old house we bought and made over to lend or rent to friends, and it was there Tony raised so many pumpkins and squash last summer. Miriam has a right of way through the place where she drives in to her house.

These small *adobe* houses that different people have bought for comparatively small amounts of money, and whitewashed and painted and cleaned up, provide all the elements for a beautiful, simple life. With a few pieces of well-designed furniture, perhaps modeled upon the Spanish Colonial and made by clever Mexican boys in the village, and mixed with two or three genuine old tables and chairs and cupboards, and with lovely colored Mexican *serapes* strewn upon the painted boards, or on the hard mud floors, and with muslin or old-fashioned checkered or sprigged calico curtains in the small-paned windows, they are picture-book houses.

Every one of them has its group of old trees to shade it, its apples or its cottonwoods; and its flower-beds in the summertime are filled with sweet peas and hollyhocks and blue larkspur.

There on the edge of the Indian pasture, then, live a group of people whose life-pattern is so different from their Mexican or Indian neighbors that it scarcely overlaps at any point, yet there is something about this valley's spaciousness, as well as its beauty, that makes it possible for these separate races to live here in amity, fundamentally indifferent to each other, superficially friendly. There is, however, one real meeting-place, and that is in their love for Taos.

In the wintertime, many of the small, remodeled houses look lifeless or asleep. They nestle in the snow; the trees about them give the sole movement in their neighborhood when the wind stirs the bare branches. No smoke rises from their cold chimneys and their windows gather a gray film of cobwebs across them. Their occupants have gone away to cities, fearful of the quiet immobility of the snow-shrouded valley, or of the enduring cold.

In Placita, Spud's house never dies. Like his Mexican neighbors', his chimneys keep their warmth all winter. In the early morning, the cock that wakens Cortez, wakens him as well; and in the night the howling dog brings him to his door shouting a fierce "Shut up!" at the same time as Enrique, across the road, tumbles out of bed to call the beast into his warm kitchen.

The "back room" in Spud's house is Rembrandtesque: all brown and black and white, from the hand press and the trays of type, the stove, the benches, the loom (where some day, we suppose, *serapes* will be woven, fusing together into odd patterns against the white walls), the dim old ceiling made of ancient cedar strips laid on beams, which comes weightily close to one's head, and the dirt floor, which provides a constant veil of fine dust that softens every outline and subdues every surface. A few numbers of past "Laughing Horses" that were born in this room, rest on shelves in their assorted colors. The room has dark corners; it has warmth, vitality, and the sense of being that places have where someone works and likes it.

There are only two other little rooms in the house. The door opens directly upon Home. Here is the diminutive cookstove with two or three small skillets and pans hanging above it and a tiny woodbox beside it—all so neat and enjoyable. In the deep embrasure of the tall, narrow window, beside the stove, geraniums bloom. The dining table is on the other side of it, covered with a red and white checkered cloth, and books and horses and more plants.

Across from the stove, there is a day bed, leaning up against a bookcase that stands out from the wall, and behind it are the pitcher and bowl, the shaving things and suchlike, and more horses along the top; horses from here, there and everywhere, for everyone sends Spud horses; horses of ivory and wood and straw, pottery horses, metal horses, laughing horses, or horses fierce and prancing, grotesque and exquisite.

Beside the door, a flashlight hangs on a nail, right at hand the moment he comes into the dark house at night. There is no electricity here, but yellow light from oil lamps that must be lighted when he comes in.

The next room, usually called the living room (though all three of these rooms are really lived in), has a tall mahogany desk with glass doors at the top and books behind them. It started, in my recollection, in my own room years ago in Buffalo, but I traded it to him for a Buffalo coat which he had, and which I wanted to give to Tony for Christmas!

There is a darling fireplace in here, of just the right size, and it has bookshelves on either side of it and horses ranging across the chimney-piece and along the tops over the books. Another tall bookcase with high glass doors, stands across the room. It came from his home, one of those things people have who have anything, that they drag along across mountains and rivers and set among the later accretions of living. The best books are in here. The sets. Spud collects books like he collects horses. He likes them for their paper, their covers, their printing and their contents. Every extra dollar he has goes for a book, and there they are, all over his three rooms. He never buys horses—they come to him —but for books he makes sacrifices.

There is another wide, low day bed in this inner room, and a drum stove that smolders all the time while he is away at the Printing Office in the village. When he comes home on a cold night, the house is warm, the lamp is soon burning, and a fresh log snapping on the embers. I have heard him describe, with the greatest sympathy in me, how cozy it is to warm up some milk and go to bed with a book and a mug of the hot drink, to feel so secure and content, alone at his ease with the wild winter shut out and nothing more to cope with till the next day!

When one thinks of the people who float around the world in hotels and boarding houses, the aging women, and men of all ages, who are looking for climates or distraction or something, they don't know what, who are without roots, and without the small household gods that give a person more heart-warming than theaters, art galleries, or any public festivity in the world, it is inconceivable that they don't know enough to find a little house somewhere that will be their very own, where every corner means something intimate and special, something planned for comfort and convenience, where the kettle sings on the hearth and the flower blooms in the window.

It is, probably, because they are afraid to be alone; but if aloneness is once confronted with courage and a final giving up and relaxing into submission, acknowledging the perpetual and essential loneliness of life, whether in crowds or in deserts, there emerges a peace and contentment in one's own small domain, and an almost tangible atmosphere of well-being that pervades it, which emanates, really, from one's own heart, coming at last home to rest.

If one could only tell some of these wanderers to come back and sit in the window and watch the clouds pass over the mountains, or to learn to cook an egg and toast on a small wood stove, and to brew a good cup of tea and drink it in a sunny room without the sound of strange voices in their ears, or the hard, cold, speculative glances of strangers' eyes exploring them in public dining rooms, one would be really doing a service. But how many would know what one meant? We cannot convey different kinds of living to each other; they must be tried out.

It was in Placita that Pooch jumped into my car one summer. I was driving up to Brett's and I saw a small black dot tearing along towards me on the road; so I stopped, and when it reached me, it sprang up over the closed door and into the seat beside me, a little black bulldog as thin as a shad, with two bat ears sticking up, and wild laughter on its face.

A Mexican girl, standing in the doorway of her house beside the road, was laughing heartily, too! I recognized the breed. Lorraine, the most beloved animal I ever had, and who died six years ago, had sprinkled her offspring over the valley. This must be out of one of the early litters, I knew. She was old and haggard, toothless and worn. Her backbone stuck out through her shabby black coat, so one could count every knob on it. Yet she laughed with gayety and a kind of racy courage, and by the strange affinity that exists between people and animals, knew me and made for me on that summer afternoon.

I wouldn't have left her for anything, so I called out to the girl who was watching us, and asked if the dog were hers—and when she said, "Yes, that's our old pooch," I asked her if she'd sell her.

The husband came along, then, and I asked how old she was. Eleven or twelve, he said. He looked amused at the idea of selling her; but Pooch had stopped laughing, herself, and was looking terribly anxious. She seemed to know her fate was being decided, and she rolled her bulbous eyes from my face to his as we talked, and she trembled all over. In her eagerness and her tenacity of living, she suddenly appeared to resemble my Grandma Ganson so strongly that the curious idea occurred to me that she *was* my grandma in another shape.

"Is she house-broken?" I asked.

"Oh, yes! She's very nice in the house," he answered. "She always sleep in that garage at night, but we keep her in the house daytimes."

"Where do you keep her in the winter?"

"Oh, same place."

"Isn't that too cold?"

"Yes, I guess so," he agreed.

Pooch gave a convulsive shake beside me.

"Well, I'll give you five dollars for her," I offered, and he nodded assent.

I started the car once more and continued on my way. Pooch sat beside me, looking perfectly at home and full of confidence. The anguished look had faded out of her face and a pleasant smile illumined it as she glanced up at me now and then.

Her eyes were unfathomably dark and wide apart and they had a blue light in them like the eyes of Duse used to have, and when she turned them on the roadside as we scurried along, they were like lenses. I liked her from the moment she joined me, and the day was more glowing and full for each of us.

Since that time, whenever we walk over to Spud's or Miriam's, and she comes along, she draws her tail in very close and lowers her head, glancing sideways, and taking mincing, light steps, as though she were trying to be invisible in that neighborhood.

Running along the frozen dirt road, Tony would reach El Prado in a few minutes. This is the next neighborhood, where some of the oldest Mexican families in the valley have lived for a long time.

Several *adobe* houses with wooden verandas, sloping wooden roofs, and dormer windows were built in the valley at one period, and some of these are to be found in El Prado. The fretwork and jigsaw decorations that adorn them, seem to have come from the same hand, though they are scattered in wide distances from each other; or perhaps they come from the same mill and were brought here to order by one of the merchants in the Sixties or Seventies and sold, piecemeal, at one of the Plaza stores.

They are crumbling, now; their patterns are breaking up; their wooden scrolls and spikes are missing like teeth in an old mouth; and these houses that once belonged to the most affluent Mexicans here, are in worse shape than the older type of *adobe* that was here before them: the plain, massive-walled house shaped like a box, with, at most, a portal supported by pine columns resting on hand-carved corbels.

They built well and they built with care those first houses in the valley. They had no nails except when they made them, so very often they went without. The heavy portals that shaded their rooms were so nicely calculated that they supported their roofs merely by their construction—with neither nails or even wooden pegs in them.

The thick round columns were topped by corbels; and along the top of the corbels went, lengthwise, squared beams that were notched to fit and join each other at the corbels' centers; then from the house wall, round beams that were thrust into the *adobe* a foot, sloped down a very little and rested on these crossbeams; and upon them, lengthwise again, went the thick, adzed boards to form the inside ceiling.

This type of porch was built to last forever. On the top

of it, the Mexicans packed dirt very hard a foot or more deep to keep out the rain; and along the edge they built a low wall of *adobes* with occasional wooden *canales* sticking out a couple of feet to carry off the rain and melted snow. The roof of the house was packed with dirt in the same way.

The people who live in these old houses now treat them differently, according to who they are. Of course some of the Mexicans who are used to sweeping the snow off their roofs so it won't melt too fast and leak into the houses, go on doing so; but the Americans who have bought them, are apt to make over the roofs, taking off the dirt and building up a secondary wooden roof that slopes an inch to a foot to let the accumulating water run swiftly off; and then upon this they lay thick rubber paper or other roofing material, and after tarring, they sprinkle fine gravel or sand thinly over it. The low wall, three or four *adobes* high, that encircles the roof, conceals this innovation, and from below the house looks flat like all the old-time buildings.

They are of the essence of homeliness and comfort, for the thick walls warm up from the fires in wintertime and keep the heat in; and keep the heat out in the summertime.

The great Mountain overlooking the valley rears up so massive and so high that the little homes scattered over the soft floor of the plain seem to be scarcely large enough for human kind to live in; and yet they are spacious enough and with lovely proportions. They nestle close to the earth and seem to be rooted in it: in fact, the earth that composes them was dug up where they stand, made into *adobe* bricks dried in the sun, and raised one upon another. The beams that support the roofs are the trees from the near-by hills; the whitewash on the walls comes from the side of a mountain over beyond Ranchos de Taos. Like the Mexicans who built them and lived in them so long, they are out of this soil and will finally return to it.

After leaving El Prado, the highway is bordered on one side by Indian farms and on the other by Mexican ones. It was not always so. In the earlier days it was all Indian land, but gradually encroachments have driven the Indians nearer to the wall of mountains that shuts in the valley on the northern side. Their tiny summer houses are dotted here and there among the fields; and when the crops are stirring, they come from the Pueblo and live in them till the harvests are in. All summer long the sound of Indian singing floats over the land as they work in the furrows, with sheets wound like huge turbans round their dark heads.

But now, in the frozen immunity of winter, the earth on either side of the road looks like blue glaciers interminably stretching to the mountain slopes, monotonously still except for a sudden splash of black, when a couple of crows land on the dark huddle of a carcass, for horses and cows fall and die throughout the cold months and are devoured in a few hours. By the time the meadows bloom again their bones, so austerely and precisely beautiful, lie bleached white with green blades pricking up through the interstices. Sometimes the pale wild iris sticks long fingers through the cavities of skull or ribs, and blooms triumphantly.

Across the wide land, Tony's little closed Ford runs smoothly, patiently making its way over to Arroyo Seco with a sack of oats in the rumble seat. He is probably singing quite loud, and thinking his deep thoughts. Out of his singing come his wise, well-considered opinions. I have never known anyone with better judgment.

He has crossed several more bridges over the mountain streams that flow down across the valley: Lucero River out of the Lucero Canyon, called Star Water by the Indians, it is so clear and cold all the year round; and the stream from the Hondo Canyon. Wherever they flow, they are bordered with the red willows and the dreaming cottonwood trees.

Already, before he reaches the place where the road curves to come in nearer to the Seco Mountain, he can see the aperture of the dark cave in its face, although the pine trees grow tall there and try to mask it: the ceremonial cave of long forgotten days, where sacrifices were made behind the waterfall that veils its recessed altar, and that Lorenzo described in "The Woman Who Rode Away."

These latter-day Indians do not like that place and will

not camp near it, nor sleep there, for they say there are bad influences hanging about it, and the spirits of evil.

A long time ago, when I first came here, I begged Tony to take me up to see it, for I was curious after what he had told me. It was winter, and the snow was on the ground, but the road was well trodden, so we could drive over with the team, for we had no car then. It took us the whole morning to reach the foot of the mountain.

We drove through the village of Arroyo Seco, a hamlet of lovely old houses, with their corrals near-by heaped with pale hay and alfalfa. The blue smoke of firesides curled merrily out of many a chimney here, and everyone seemed to be inside except two or three boys who stood outside the Pool Hall with muffled ears and rosy cheeks.

There seemed to be geraniums blooming in every little window.

"What a lovely place! I'd like to live here," I cried.

Seco, a little community under the rocky north wall of a round mountain, exposed to all the sunshine and overlooking the sloping valley—it really breathed of coziness and contentment, like a cat purring in the sun.

But Tony said: "Maybe you'd get lonesome pretty quick. Winter is long over here." But I thought not.

We drove on along its only road, then left it behind us as we began to walk the horses on the slope up the hill.

We ate our lunch at noon beside the stream that trickles

down out of the pool below the waterfall. With blankets wrapped around our knees, we sat on a fallen tree and drank coffee that Tony made over a small fire; and he cooked a beefsteak that he held in a crotched stick.

The sun was warm, and there was a green edging of turf beside the brook and all about us grew ranks of perfect little Christmas trees that climbed the slope. While we ate, our horses munched oats from nose bags that hung from their ears; and it was so clear and still and remote that it seemed to me we were the only people in the world. Little animals squeaked and chirped and Tony made noises to call them and they answered, cautiously, the squirrels and woodchucks and other small things.

When we were through eating and ready to start walking up to the cave (for we had to leave our buggy down below), Tony looked at the unbroken snow between the trees and he said:

"Maybe we better not go."

But I was eager to get started and I persuaded him, so he took his gun and we began to plod along the trail that he knew but that I couldn't see at all.

I walked behind him, trying to fit my feet into his tracks, but the snow got deeper and deeper, so that first it came in over the tops of my arctic overshoes and wet my skirts, and then soaked me to my knees; but we kept on through the Christmas trees until they turned into tall pines that darkened the way so that it seemed more like evening than early afternoon.

The stream grew wider as we climbed up the side of the mountain, and once Tony stopped and told me to listen and we could hear the noise it made falling over the top of the cave into the pool below—a muffled roar that sounded like a noise in a dream.

Once in a while there was a sudden tremendous threshing of wings above us, and some huge bird would rise heavily out of a tree top and swoop away. Probably I imagined it, but the woods seemed to grow sinister and haunted and to lose the lightsome feeling they had down below.

We wound around a hillock and the steepness made me hot and breathless, though it was very cold in the deep shade of the trees.

Suddenly Tony said: "The cave is just ahead," and I saw a tall pine that spread its branches across the face of some brown, craggy rocks.

We skirted the harsh walls of stone, and the noise of falling water was deafening. Soon we could see it, falling from above our heads. It splashed icy drops that coated everything near with a covering like steel, and it fell upon a thick column of green ice that had gradually reared itself up out of the basin below it.

The water ran down the sides of the monstrous, transparent pillar of ice, congealing and thickening it; and what escaped formed a dark pool at the base and ran out at one end to filter down the hill away from that grim place behind the trees, until it reached sunlight and happier things.

Tony led the way in behind the water to the shadowy cave. The light came in green and subdued and we found a large, dry chamber of rock with a high, domed ceiling, and with the sides sloping upwards to meet it. He showed me where there were steps, apparently roughly hewn out at the back wall, leading up to a ledge; and above the ledge and far above us, impossible to reach without a long ladder, there was the faint painting of a sun.

"Rising in the east," Tony said; and true enough, it was at the point where the sun comes over the mountains in the middle of winter.

I began to climb up the side of the cave and he followed. We reached the flat ledge and sat on it and from up there we looked across the dim room to the ice-column, and beyond its green transparency to the pine tree sentinel outside. The tree tops beyond were massed and thick, but between the branches we could see far, far away to the western horizon and the dazzling, white, sunny valley; and up there where we were, it was entirely different from the life down below, which sparkled and shone and laughed—for here a brooding spirit dwelt in eternal gloom and im-

VILLAGE STREET (*photograph by Ernest Knee*)

NEW CHURCH AT TAOS PUEBLO *(photograph by Ansel Adams)*

mobility, save for the irrevocable fall of the water past the entrance.

I shivered and Tony said: "This not a nice healthy place. Better go before you catch cold," and he took my hand and helped me climb down the steep rock wall. Together, somewhat in haste, we left; and the life that lingered there paid no heed to our going, but seemed to gaze vastly over and beyond us to the west, where the sun would soon go down in the tender sky.

We ran almost all the way down through the heavy snow, and I fell once or twice and when we reached the peaceful horses, I was soaked through. Tony snatched the blankets off them and put on their bridles and hurried us to the house of a Mexican friend who lived below. It was one of the first human habitations we reached, and it lay on the upper slopes, outside the village.

When Tony knocked at the door, the woman who had watched us eagerly from the window, opened it, smiling with pleasure.

"Friend," said Tony in Spanish, "this lady is all damp. By a favor, let her come in and dry her stockings and shoes, please."

"Surely. Come in," cried the woman, and hustled us into two chairs in front of the fireplace.

I took off my wet things and stretched my cold, red feet out to the blaze. Our friend looked expectant, but she was too polite to ask questions. Tony glanced at her from a corner of his eyes and hesitated before he told her. Then he said:

"Been taking a little walk to the cave up above."

"Oh, to the cave?" she responded with a polite social manner, but throwing a curious glance over me, apparently to see if I had any remnants of its alien atmosphere still clinging to me. I smiled at her. The situation needed loosening up, somehow, for Tony was acting rather formal, it seemed, and covering up something.

"Yes, looking for bear tracks," he continued.

"Oh?" she returned, politely. "Did you find any?"

"Oh, yes," he went on in a singsong voice. "Like in winter." He looked at the stove in the corner where several stew pots simmered under lids.

"Got hot chili?" he queried, mostly as if to change the subject.

"Surely! I pray you have some chili and coffee."

"I don't care if I do," he answered in the equivalent Spanish, and she set dishes out on a table that had an oil-cloth on it depicting George Washington standing on the White House steps.

"Better eat some," he said to me. "Very good for cold."

He was breaking a *tortilla* and he ladled up the chili with it. I moved over, timidly, not liking to refuse, for I was

92

still, at that time, under the sway of a collection of taboos that had been taught me by Americans, when I came to this country; taboos that had arisen in their own prejudices, for instance, never refuse anyone's food or it will seem to be a reflection on it and would hurt his feelings. This isn't true. The people who live here are at home and at their ease. They feel independent and sure of themselves, and nothing we can do or not do ever shakes their security, for they are not so sensitive to us as we hope. If we do not eat with them, it is because our tastes are different, and each is welcome to his own.

These small conventional habits of dealing with either Mexicans or Indians are generally penetrated with more tolerance and humor than we think. There was one old governor at the Pueblo who got so used to the formula that Americans served up to him that once when I took a friend from New York in to call, he smiled benignly when he took her hand and he said, anticipating her rhetoric before she had a chance:

"You have come a long, long way over the land and the rivers and mountains to visit the Indians? Very far? Yes." He looked down from his height and beamed kindly, but his eyelids were a little weary.

We sat at the table a while, and Tony and the Mexican woman finally got off on a good old exchange of gossip about crops and the news of Seco. I looked around the room and saw some beautiful things mingled with the ordinary objects we manufacture for the use of such as she was. There was a lovely, innocent Santo hanging over a hideous brass bed; a painting of Toby, the fisherman. He was round-cheeked and young and he had a string of mountain trout in one hand. St. Tobias is just the proper saint for these villages that straggle alongside the streams. In the corner there stood a beautiful, mellow-looking carved chest, shiny with handling and not with Johnson's wax, like our furniture.

"Look, Tony," I broke in, "look at that nice chest! I wish we could get it."

He got up and went over and looked skeptically down at it. I saw he thought it was too old, but he said, to oblige me: "The granary?"

"Yes, sir," the woman answered, and lifted up the lid. Inside we saw lying the clean golden wheat, three or four hundred pounds of it.

"Maybe you like to trade the old box?" Tony queried.

The woman put her head on one side and smiled.

"Oh, surely," she sang, softly. "What does the lady want to give me for it?"

"Oh, maybe a new trunk from the store," Tony sang in reply.

This melodic duet went on up and down a tuneful scale until the chest was mine, and he promised to come back some day with a brand new trunk from the Plaza and take the old one away with him in the buggy.

"I don't know what you want with them old Mexican things," he grumbled when we were driving home. "Maybe full of *chinchi*, and smell bad, too, of beans!"

"Oh, I *love* them," I cried. For me they were rich and stable, their aroma was precious and their slowly-gathered charm was secure and spell-binding; but for Tony, who did not need these qualities, because his life was made up of them already, the fascination in objects lay more in their clean-cut, practical use. I know he loved a shiny new trunk from the store, with a good lock and key that worked, just as much better than this greasy, old, battered box I craved, as the Mexican woman did. That is how, here in this valley, we are shifting things around, and exchanging values.

Well, from my window now I could see the Seco Mountain, and just about where the cave was, scooped out of the side of it; and while I lay there remembering that first winter day we went up there, I knew Tony must be remembering it, too, as he drove towards it. The carved box was in the dining room, below, and another one like it that must have been made by the same man, so alike they are. The house is filled with things that remind me of journeys and expeditions Tony and I took together all over the country.

Beyond the round hump of Seco Mountain, and across the deep indenture of Hondo Canyon, I saw the twin peaks of Lobo Mountain, and the small, bare patch, low down in the pines of the hillside, that is the Lawrence ranch.

How cold and deserted it must be up there, with Frieda away for the winter! The snow must be piled in drifts against the porch, and the wind making a deep humming in the trees, and the chipmunks and the pack rats, with their long angora tails, have possession of the place to their hearts' content, for Frieda's two black cats are left with Scott to take care of.

I wish she were there right now! I miss her zestfulness, her warm exuberance and life that animates the whole mountain for one, when one drives up to see her and she comes, crying "helo-o-o!" from her porch, wrinkling up her nose and opening her mouth in a shout of delight, and showing her strong, white teeth.

But she is part of the summer and autumn life, like others. I must remember it is winter, now, and there are only a handful of us left here, and we make up our days with fewer pleasures and at a closer range. We stay in the house more, and the changing light in a room, falling first on one portion of it, and then on another as the day passes quietly, has a kind of experience in it, a feeling of deep living that we miss in the freedom of movement that comes when the frost is out of the ground.

I always knit in the wintertime, and I can't endure doing that in the summer! But as soon as the days grow shorter, I hunt for my bag of wools and all my amber needles, and I am perfectly content to sit in the window and knit and knit and knit and ponder and remember and get into a kind of even rhythm of thinking, feeling, breathing, knitting; that is, somehow, a very satisfactory activity, like a dance, or like the slow, sure motion of a constant star.

Out of this purring intensity there are produced many little sweaters. Not being proficient in sleeves or necks, they are merely slip-ons with a hole at the top and two holes for the arms. All over the Pueblo they can be seen every winter on the little boys. Turquoise blue, pink, emerald green, sapphire, red, they are dots of bright color running against the snow. At the beginning, they are of a fair proportion, coming to below the waist, but with each washing they grow longer and longer, so finally they come well below the knees and look like cylinders—but nobody seems to mind!

I was watching a little cloud floating over the Sacred Mountain, no bigger than a man's hand, as the saying goes, when I heard Mrs. Gonzales' deprecating voice once more.

"Pardon, *Señora*, but Max says the cellar is full of water!"

Oh, merciful heavens! Again? Why does one try to have plumbing in such a country! Always, always there's something going wrong with it.

"Well, I'll come down and telephone Mr. Vickrey," I answered, in an aggrieved voice, as one is apt to do to a messenger of evil tidings.

Slipping on my quilted dressing-gown and my quilted slippers, I climbed the seven steps up out of my peaceful room and padded rather angrily, I am afraid, across the sunny gray floor beyond, went down a step onto a landing that was stained in bright colors from the imitation stained-glass windows Brett painted in the bathroom that opened upon it, went down twelve steps, turned and went down six more to the small, dark library where all the books that line two walls stand staring out and wondering if anyone will ever read them again.

The silent house was perfumed with the dry cedar that is burned in it every morning; a small branch is lighted and blown out, and the smoke permeates the rooms and makes a most clean and peaceful smell. In the big room everything sparkled in the somber way that dark, waxed furniture and colored glass and copper bowls will do when they are set in order and dusted. I always think a room never looks so attractive all day long as just after it is cleaned in the morning, the cushions patted out, and the water changed in the flower vases, waiting and ready and renewed for living in again, fresh every day.

My house can always mollify me when I feel cross; just to walk through it again and find it so sweet and clean sets one in order when one is thrown out of gear. So a disorderly and neglected house must put one down, I think, and untune one, no matter how happy one might be, and make one feel life is not worth living for its dreariness and effort.

I heard a small moan from Pooch, who was lying on the couch upon a yellow cushion and knew what was coming.

"You get off there," I called, as I swept her to the floor in my passage.

"Oh, all right," she groaned, and removed herself to the fireplace.

"Mr. Vickrey, the cellar's full of water," I called down the telephone.

"All right," he answered in a pleased, anticipatory voice. "I'll be right up!"

"Tcha! Tcha!" said Beatrice. "There certainly does always seem to be something the matter with that plumbing! Now you're here," she went on, "you'd better order some of that dog food. The cans are all gone."

"Oh, Beatrice! Why didn't you tell me before they were

finished? You know I have to telephone to Santa Fe for them, and then wait days!"

"Well, seems like I just forgot," she pleaded, sorry.

I knew, once I emerged, there would be all kinds of things. . . .

I telephoned Kaune's and then I went back to the other end of the house, and groped my way down the cellar stairs. I may know something about how things run on the upper levels of my house but pipes defeat me. I just don't know one thing about heating systems, plumbing systems, cesspools, septic tanks, or why electricity makes things run!

There must be many who would see a fearful symbolism here, for I do myself. However, before I am through living, I will doubtless be forced to catch up with this aspect of life and complete myself, as I believe I have in some other ignorances I was born with. If not, perhaps I will have to return to this earth and be a plumber! (Lord, help me to learn to cope with it now!)

Fearfully, I looked down into the small, dark cellar. The floor was covered with water, I didn't know how deep; it looked somewhat like Manby's Hot Springs looks from the ladder when we descend it. A continuous cheerful splashing was going on, so I knew it was still running in somewhere.

I only took one look and ran up the stairs. We were all

in Mr. Vickrey's hands, now! I could do nothing. I kept on going up and down stairs until I was finally back in my own room with the door shut, and then I heard Mr. Vickrey's truck rush up below the east window and I ran over to put my head out in the frosty air.

"What *do* you think is the matter with it now?" I cried down to him. He looked up, smiling happily. He is large and pink-faced, with blue eyes, and on Sundays he looks like a daguerreotype.

"Well, I guess one of the joints on a valve has come loose from the main stack that leads to the septic tank," he glibly answered—or something like that. "I can't say till I get *to* it," and he made for the back door.

He likes knowing more than people know about their own plumbing. All right, I thought, let him; and I went back to bed and looked out of the window, and I found that small cloud had grown large and larger and rested on the taller peak of the mountain, now, like a cap, and that made my heart sink a little, for it meant a snowstorm.

It was just the same as in Florence, when we saw a cloud come down on the tallest of the Apennines across the way. The Florentines had a saying for it:

> *Quando Monte Morello tiene capello,*
> *Fiorentino prende ombrello.*

There would be a new layer of snow over the land before many hours had passed, and we would be bound in firmer, the iron frost in the ground would deepen, and in the early morning the rime would coat every branch and twig and stiffen the pale stubble in the fields.

Something like a shiver went over me at the thought of the winter thickening still more, covering us, clamping us down, until I remembered what I learned long ago, but always forget and have to learn anew each year: that if one gives up and lets it come right down over one, if one sinks into the season and is a part of it, there is peace in this submission. Only in resistence there is melancholy and a sort of panic.

It doesn't take long for the aspect of the world to change here, and in a short time great galleons of cloud sailed over the sky and soon covered the sun. Then everything looked sad indeed. We depend so much on the high key of light for illumining things.

When the sun shines, it colors every tree and hummock of earth near-by and in the distance the ether seems of ponderable blue and violet and mauve; the mountain changes from pansy purple to periwinkle blue, and great cloud-shadows shaped like eagles move over it, or it turns ink black splashed with white, behind the pale, radiant fields that glisten and flash. All day long there are changes of color and mood, startling and strange, and one never grows accustomed to the endless variety of the hours.

But when the sun is gone, the earth looks widowed and

drear. The winter fields seem shabby and dirty, splashed with manure and trodden into dinginess by the horses. The Mountain shrinks and crouches until it seems only half as high as usual, and it loses all its majesty. The landscape might be in New England instead of on a high and halcyon tableland in a region of magic.

So, on this morning, the lovely world turned gray and folded itself inward so its face was hidden—and I drew the curtain over the window and, to hearten myself, I thought of my friends who live beside a blue ocean with a field of wild flowers behind them; of my friend who lives in a little apartment in a city whose windows are covered with lace and whose living room is all a soft shine of Venetian glass and old, carved gold, and who always keeps faith; and of that fabulous couple whose island is always blessed, where the fruit and flowers follow each other unendingly and every meal is eaten in a grassy corner beside running water.

On such days as this one turned into, I go back to those I have perhaps forgotten a little on the surface, though I do hold them always secure underneath and never truly forget them.

These are the days when all the letters get written: the crisp paper rustles and the pen travels over the sheets until the row of envelopes is in a long file on the table, side by side, addressed and stamped.

This morning, then, I was away in California, in New

York, Russia, Mexico and Austria, and even in Prague. The hours slipped away and everything near-by was forgotten until Mrs. Gonzales appeared once more with a blue tray in her hands.

"It is the lunch, *Señora*," she said, apologetically.

I fell upon it with great zest. Cold beef with homemade horseradish, potato salad, muffins, tea, and preserved quinces.

"How about the plumbing?"

"Well, that man, he found it and he fix it, and he hauled all the water out of there," she answered, with a mystified look. "The telephone lady called just now, and says there's a telegram," she went on, "and Jose wants to know, will you order some shoes and he will fix the horses this afternoon."

I didn't want to get up and go downstairs again and plunge into things. This was an off-day, when I had meant to keep myself to myself, so I began to sneeze. Not on purpose. The sneezes came spontaneously, one after another, and I could not stop them.

"Oh, *Señora!*" exclaimed Mrs. Gonzales in a horrified voice. "Are you warm enough? Do you feel a draught?"

"Of course, I feel a draught!" I answered, laughing. I always feel a draught; this room is a cave of the winds from all these windows, but they generally don't affect me. In fact, I like a room that is full of cool breezes and warmth from the stove or the fireplace. The freesia in the vase beside the bed always tremble, imperceptibly, in the moving air of the room.

"No, Mrs. Gonzales, I'm sneezing because I don't want to go and telephone. But I'll be down as soon as I've eaten," I concluded, with a feeling of worth and virtue. For every single time I have to attend to anything, whether it's a horse, or a telegram from goodness knows who, or a hole in the wall, or getting the windows washed, it is a distinct effort, like climbing a hill; and I suppose that is why I've built up all these rooms and gathered all these animals around me, for one lives by instinctively creating the means to develop the weak places in oneself, and out of the effort to deal with them in continuity comes order and peace and the feeling of relationship, without which one may as well be dead and, in fact, is dead.

I pulled the curtain away from the window and looked out while I was eating. The mountain was gone. Only the silver beeches near the kitchen showed through the veils of snow that were falling with steady persistence. Well, it would be a perfect afternoon for Samuel Johnson! But I felt uneasy at the thought of Tony over there in Arroyo Seco, separated by a thick wall of snow that might pile high before nighttime, and I hoped he'd try to get home before the dark came down.

When I was telephoning, I called up Helen and asked her to come up and have tea with me, but she said:

"Well, maybe, but your road will be terrible by teatime if this goes on, and my chains aren't on."

"What are you doing?" I asked.

"I'm making a cake from that recipe of Myrtle's. You know, the one you make with pecans and pineapple. And I thought I'd try to cut out that piece of silk Martha sent me."

I was with her in her wide living room where the fire snoozed in the chimney; I knew her house smelled sweet with sugar and butter and spices, and that probably she'd swept all Doctor's letters and newspapers onto the window-sill, and had her silk unfolded on the round table.

"Oh, do come over later," I begged. "I know I'm going to have a broken heart by teatime! I have a Cold."

"You *have?* I didn't think you ever caught cold."

"I don't, generally."

"Well, I'll try, only don't expect me till you see me."

I tried Spud at the Printing Office and tried my luck with him; but, oh, dear, I'd forgotten it was Thursday and he had to stay late and get the paper out.

As I stood there, a man knocked at the kitchen door. The sheep had arrived that Tony ordered on his way that morning. It lay in a small truck, and it was neatly wrapped in a canvas. Its feet were tied together and its interior yawned like a cavern. In a gunny-sack were all the things that had been extracted from inside it: heart, liver, kidneys, stomach and guts. We would have liver and bacon and kidney pie, and the other things Tony would give the Indians, and they would use them for all kinds of purposes, for tanning and making different articles. The skin would be washed and softened and turned into a small covering for the floor. Nothing is wasted in this country.

Beatrice wears the key of the meat room around her neck on a string. She yanked it out and accompanied the Mexican to the dark, cold chamber, and he hung the sheep up on a hook and I returned to the upper regions and put a big log into the stove.

"To write the Life of him who excelled all mankind in writing the lives of others, and who, whether we consider his extraordinary endowments, or his various works, has been equaled by few in any age, is an arduous and may be reckoned in me a presumptuous task. . . ."

I read on and on. By the time I reached page 557, I was so depressed that I could read no more. The poor old man who was counted wise in his time seems negative to us today, and that we hold to be the dullest sin we know. The pages of notes on his travels in France, running like this:

. . . To Versailles, a mean town. Carriages of Business passing. Mean shops against the wall. . . ." I pressed on until I reached the words: "The moat of the Bastille is dry. . . ." and there I threw the book on the floor. . . .

Perhaps my restlessness came from more than impatience with Sam Johnson. The room was darkening and growing chilly. I had forgotten the stove while I was lost in the thick volume, and now it was late in the afternoon.

The white snow on the ground was reflected up onto the ceiling through the windows, and most of the light in the room was up there shining in a feeble, livid kind of way in the corners, a look that Lorenzo always used to hate and speak of in the wintertime. The house was utterly still below me, and I felt lonesome and drear. How glad I would be when spring would be here, I thought, remembering how it would come all at once. . . .

Suddenly, one evening, there is a new light on earth. One had grown accustomed to the closing in of night before the afternoon was over, so that people could hardly see each other's faces when they passed in the street outside the post office; and then comes a twilight when it is not the same.

The sky rises and is loosed in a vast, warm, sighing heave. The village is bathed in a dark, tender gloaming that is suffused with moist easiness, and the mountains that show at the end of every road in this place, have lost their hardness.

They seem to breathe and stretch, looming higher and higher.

We ourselves are permeated with the blessed change and something gives in us. We cry to each other as we pass: "Just like spring, isn't it?" And men cease to walk with heads bent to keep the warmth of themselves inside their collars. They lift their faces and look about them, and everybody is able to recognize and share this marvel. Their bones and blood vibrate and flow with the season's rhythm; for a moment they are one with it. The new light comes like a breath that enlivens and lifts the dull, sleepy earth and it glows inside men, shining in their eyes.

Everything looks larger in this warm flood; it expands houses, horses, and even hearts. It is still a darkling twilight, but it is fuller and more fluid, for the tight winter sky is suffused with moisture and thin pink clouds float airily across the dusky broken dome. Like cold eyes that have forgotten the warmth of tears, the winter sky feels the sweet melancholy of renewal, and the ability to pour itself out with ease and ecstasy.

People sniff the air, thinking they can smell flowers, then they go home to supper and provoke each other into quarrels which are followed by tears, and they mingle their juices in the warm liquid reconciliations of spring. This is the first of the spring cleanings. Follows then the house-cleaning, with furniture out in front yards, and winter clothes, sometimes prematurely, hung out on the line to air before being put away in moth-balls.

One lives from month to month all the year round, forgetting the future and what it will be like; then when it comes, with icicles and iris, sheaves of corn or violets in the shade, one's eternal recognition meets it with the same wonder and surprise. There is nothing so new in all eternity as this old earth, reborn every day like ourselves, and never twice the same, impossible to remember out of season, yet intense with premonition.

The birds are ready at the first hint of the convenient relaxation in the air. They appear. Instead of only an occasional lonely lark, sitting on a fence post and singing in an atmosphere of closed frigidity, there they are all around, yellow-breasted, pouring fluid music out into the hospitable sunshine.

In the spring my room gets warm early, and is full of a glaring yellow light and I must get up and draw the curtains and make it dim so I can sleep on for a while, but this will not be for long because the English sparrows in all the trees outside my windows keep up a shrill outcry. They are the most pestiferous things! They drive away all the lovely wild ones, the bluebirds, the wind birds, the canaries, and others, and they take possession of the place. From dawn on, all day long, they fill the air with the noisy, excitable, insensitive sounds of their activities! Urging the young ones to leave the nests and fly, quarreling, disputing over the best places on the trees, driving each other about; and once the babies have left the nests, how they carry on! Shrieking in fear and fluttering their short wings, afraid to try the journey back to the nest, hopping up and down with open beaks, panicky, hungry. Cheep! Cheep! Cheeping for food!

I have tried to get rid of the sparrows, but without success. A friend told me of sparrow traps. One baits a kind of wire cage with a trail of grain that leads into a funnel-shaped opening and they all go in at the wide end and then cannot find the way out. When the trap is full, one's hired man carries it away and disposes of the catch. How? One wonders and tries not to think much about it. I know a man who lives here in the summertime and suffers from these pests but has never done anything about them. He is a man who likes the quiet in a shaded room on a warm afternoon, and outside in the sunny patio their slummy noise would drown out the serenity of the Bach Fugue, destroying the illusion of peace. I told him I had heard of traps and asked him to look them up somewhere, for us both, when he went East; so he asked the Agricultural Department to send me information about them. It did. It sent me a list of sixty firms distributed all over the United States that dealt in birds, pets, their destruction and culture and among them was listed, in particular, English sparrows and the means to get rid of them. I wrote hopefully to ten of these addresses, asking for details and prices, and not one of them replied. So I gave up! (*"Que vivre est difficite! Oh mon cœur fatigué!"*)

Everything likes each other, now, the sky leans tenderly to the earth and the birds adore the sun, the fields begin to palpitate and to steam, and green things prick and break through. The moist manure has a delicate perfume that comes in the open window; it suggests hyacinths and jonquils and one's heart opens to it.

Soon, soon one can look for the rake and the hoe and the old, rusty trowel, and it is delicious to get out of doors soon after breakfast and begin to work in the garden. The sun is hot on one's back and it is not long before the pores open and little streams run along one's limbs and under one's hair. Like all else in Nature now, one turns more fluid, melting and dissolving. But the spring gardening is more a beginning than a continuous activity. I don't like gardening, really, though I love flowers so much. No, it is just to help things along, to give a push to it all, that every spring one gets the need to touch and break and loosen up the earth around the struggling plants. When they are through and coming up strong, let Max take care of them. This mid-wifery is latent in all women and we are, every one of us, always aching to deliver the unborn, if not in ourselves, then outside ourselves in some vicarious fashion.

The stiff green iris shoots spear the hard earth that clasps their bulbous roots in a vice. Nothing will stay these harbingers from their appointed bloom. Along the Acequia Madre they border the garden planted there; they outline the lawn; they encircle the young trees. Before the grass is green, they pierce the air with small, vivid shrieks of green music.

The trees are more reluctant. Until one feels them with one's hands, one does not know for sure that they still live. But take the branch and bend it, and then assurance comes, for it is flooded with the same life that runs in one's fingers. Fluid, the sap is coursing along the channels like blood that will find its way, and if one clips with the big pruning shears, it gushes out, as like as not falling on one's face like a cool hemorrhage, for the trees are not hot, like we are, nor are any of these earth lives burning like us with the electric velocity of flesh and bone, though the tension of their growth is no less than ours.

The sap runs incontinently out of the opened veins. The inertia of winter has been overcome and the trees are drawing their water up out of the earth. It runs down the trunk of the tree, darkening it. If one has cut too much, from ignorance, or from sheer delight, the tree will bleed to death.

"I 'fraid that tree goin' to dry up," said Tony, looking at a small mountain ash I had been working on. In the sunlight, the tree stood glistening and moist. It dripped and lost its essence, which was falling slowly back onto the ground and soaking in to where it had come from.

I remembered the vines in the vineyard below the Villa Curonia when the *contadino* cut each twig in the spring and where, for days, a drop shone at every severed artery. "The vines are weeping," said Pietro; but they did not die for that. Their weeping set them in motion and brought the new grapes, as so often with men, when sorrow cuts them to the quick and a new growth starts burgeoning from the inert blood stream, set once more in motion.

Wait—and presently a green flush binds the top of the cottonwoods together, though as yet no single leaf can be seen upon them. Life is flushing everything, washing green color onto the tree tops and across the feathers of the bluebirds turning them from gray to indigo. The yellow brightens across the lark, and the Sacred Mountain grows soft as a purple plum.

Too slow for God, this dream-like, deliberate approach! He sends his winds and the valley bends under the assault that comes booming up from the south, hurling dry tumbleweeds over the desert like bubbles, burying us in a cloud of yellow dust that gets into our hair and skin, that is grit in the mouth and harsh on the floor under our feet. A fine layer of *adobe* is on everything in every house in this place; it seeps between the pages of books; and it lies upon the cream in the ice-box!

And it shakes the leaves loose on the trees. The apple trees are budded, the red is running out of them into rosy nipples and soon the lilacs will be in bloom.

The pigeons dip and circle around the house, flying against the gale, and they seem to exult all the more for the vastness of it. The dogs whine at the door to be let in, Pooch looking disgruntled and disillusioned, for spring no longer thrills her old carcass, nor sends her alertly sniffing out a likely mate in neighbors' gardens. She has dust on her nose, and her eyes are bloodshot.

Oh, Robin! How red your breast is! You listen smartly at the grassy gate of the ground for worms turning in their sleep! Is it not too soon?

("The March winds do blow, and we shall have snow, and what will poor Robin do then, poor thing?")

But we cannot wait—none of us can wait for life. We take a chance, every year the same chance, and every year our impatience betrays us.

"Max, you can uncover the garden; rake off the manure and dead leaves. Clean it all up."

"Isn't it too soon?" he asks, with wisdom's indifference.

"Oh, I don't think it's going to be cold any more," I answer, wishfully.

"No?"

He rakes away the winter bedding and the tender daffodils show their low yellow heads beneath the thick blanket of leaves. The narcissi are up, the pansies are luxuriant under the north window where he has to lift a solid mass of frozen manure and leaf-mold off them. In the patio, the hollyhock plants are as big as cabbages and they are pressing up between the flagstones of the courtyard, seedlings from last year. The delphiniums are bunchy clumps of green, and the oriental poppies look like artichoke plants.

How lovely to get them out once more! It has been lonesome without the garden. I lose interest in the plants that have been by me in the house, even in the yellow lily, with white-spotted leaves that I have been watching grow up from a bright flower into a white-spotted leaf itself.

Even in the primroses and in the cyclamen, with their little bonnets and their sweet, acrid smell; and in the plants that were presents and have taken on something of their donors' personalities as I watched them, day by day, putting out new leaves and flowers. This is not exactly an inconstancy—but rather a widening of love, a reaching out for more flowers, more and more flowers, and more love.

When the wind drops at sunset, the thermometer drops with it, from fifty to ten above zero. The night is clear and the moon shines a little yellow through the dust hanging in the air. When I wake up at dawn, I hang out the window, open on my cold pillow. How quiet, how quiet and cold it is! Where is the spring that one had already grown so used to? Winter, forgotten, is back again; the little plants down there have been nipped and blackened by frost. It makes one's heart sink and discourages one with everything; and though it is one's own impatience that has made a premature covenant with March, that would have been weathered more suitably in April, that does not console one. As in the growth of love and friendship, when the flux and flow of relationship moves with its own momentum too slowly, and one uncovers the roots in eagerness to reach the flower, the bitter fruit of untimely haste and the arresting of love by shock and an unseasoned hurry, are no more easy to endure because the fault is one's own.

Now the garden had a setback, and one could only wait and see if there was enough energy in the little plants to begin all over again: new leaves, new buds, a whole new effort to come into being.

And would this teach me anything? No, I would do the same thing again next year. Perhaps the fact that the garden manages to survive every time, has something to do with this. Like love, the earth is strong and resourceful, and suffer as it may from my presumption, it can take it and go on. If this were not so, we would not adore it as we do, for it is the steadfast power and plenty that proves it beyond our destruction, that will enable it to proceed long after we are gone, that awakens our trust and our security and clasps us closer than any human love can hold us. . . .

When the grass is green and the iris are moving purple and quiet, like women gossiping with their heads together, it is hard to remember the deep, woolly snow and how hard it is to walk through it in the winter.

Tony and I used to go out hunting together sometimes when there was a new snowfall. Then the fresh tracks showed up where the animals had passed and the way they went. Tony would go on ahead through the woods, breaking a trail, and I would try to follow in his steps.

A still wood, with the new white covering, can be wonderful and as though the earth were remade that day; and the trees, standing bowed a little by the weight they have to bear until a wind comes that will shake it off, seem patient and trustful.

On the ground we saw many little writings, left delicately by the animals, lovely patterns in a rhythm of movement and ease, soft as the imprint of waves upon the sand, sensitive as the record of the heartbeat, written by the electrocardiograph.

One day in particular that I remember, Tony was tracking a deer. The hard, cleft marks of the hooves sprang upward in pairs, showing how he had run through the trees. Tony moved more rapidly and ever more silently, holding his gun in both hands, and I thought we would never come to the end of it, it was such hard going in the snow; but all of a sudden there was a flurry and a flapping ahead of us, high up in a pine tree. An eagle rose, head low, and heavily climbed into the sky between the thick branches; and the minute Tony saw it, he raised his gun with an involuntary movement and fired. He missed, and another sound followed the report of the gun. Ahead of us somewhere, we heard the quick crackle of broken twigs and the hasty departure of an animal running.

Tony gave an exclamation of impatience. "I so stupid!" he said in a low voice.

"Why? What was it?" I asked him, not understanding what had taken place.

"That eagle saw us coming first, and got up to warn the deer!" he said. "See? Here is where the deer was lying down, and the eagle, she was up on the tree."

"Do you mean to say that that eagle made you fire your gun so the deer would know we were close?"

"Yes, she made us tell, *some* way, we comin'. The eagle always take care of the deer. . . ." And he told me of other friendships between the wild animals and how they help each other. When he tells me things, it seems to me there is as much of coöperation as there is of cruelty in that world, and we usually think only of the cruel side of their habits, and how they prey upon each other and live in perpetual fear. We know very little.

But how changeable the weather is in the spring—it is poetic and passionate by turns! It makes us fanciful and full of queer impulses. The wind starts to blow again, and we shut ourselves inside the house at the far end, away from the southwest gale that disrupts and rouses a frenzy in us; while outside, the branches of the trees toss and weave together, trying to overcome the fate of trees, which is to stay in one place and never walk or run away; and the water courses down from the mountain lakes in numberless streams, laughing at the challenge.

In the spring, there is a black panther hidden behind all the appearances of Nature. He crouches in us when we are at bay among the chairs and tables of houses; he is clinging to the tree tops and lashing out, teeth bared among the young leaves, and he is riding down the streams on the sparkling brown water, sleek and black with the white light in his eyes.

He is the master. Out of his ruthless ferocity there pours the soft foam of wild plum blossoms all over the valley; the orchards are pink and blond with the beneficence borne

TAOS GIRL (*photograph by Carl Van Vechten*)

TAOS PUEBLO (*photograph by Edward Weston*)

out of his cruelty; and along the borders of the garden, the large purple iris blossoms touch their heads together gently and breathe out a perfume that fills all our rooms; and each flower carries a drop of the stinging blood of the black panther in its heart.

Every day the leaves widen on the branches. They are shining with newness and there is a sticky feeling to some of them where the sap exudes through the delicate skin. The leaves smell strongly with the undisguised odors of the inner earth. They have the odors of men and of women when they are natural and moist with their own juices, the perfumes of the flesh that are indistinguishable from the sweet and stinking perfumes of the soil, and that are, all of them, the oxidations of the black panther who is at home within them all.

Young cottonwood leaves and sage, mint and leeks and onions breathe out of our pores the essences of the same earth as well as roses and hyacinths do, the unmitigated, solitary ecstasy of living. Like the salt of the sea in our blood stream, is the soil of the earth in our flesh, and the black panther who animates the wheat field, rides in us also in triumph; and if we, struggling in our Christian coil, succeed in casting him out, he prowls behind us, waiting an entrance, for there is not one too many for him in this universe, and he needs every blade of grass and every faltering human being, to carry him along.

When the valley is white with blossoms and all sweet with fragrance, a new sound mingles with the early morning singing of the meadow larks. Doleful and bereft, the lowing of the cows who have dropped their calves and had them taken away. . . .

The mild morning air is still when the wind ceases, and every movement that breaks it comes to one lying in peace beside the open window. The turkeys gobble-gobble over in the corral, and hark-hark the lark far up in the blue, excited small birds twitter in a thousand leafy branches and Jose chops wood. Into this spring dawning sounds Moo-o-o, moo-o-o, anguishing and broken-hearted, and the piebald cow hangs her head over the sagging gray gate and gives voice to agony.

The little calf is hanging by its feet on the iron hook, its head is severed, and soon we will be restoring ourselves with its tender cutlets.

The white foam of the warm milk is carried down into the pail by coarse, hard hands, draining it out; and the black panther hides in the shrill, alternate streams—another exit for him, and another entrance, in an hour at breakfast time.

All over the valley the young animals drop from the mothers who carried them through the cold months. What instant, immediate life! A lamb is squeezed out of the hot womb, lies a moment while the mother licks it, then it is up on its long, weak, untried legs, wavering and wondering. It looks around a little foolishly from eyes that still have the look of the inner earth, when all of a sudden it will give a tiny bleat and seem to smile and leap right up into the air, apparently with the joy of being there. I wonder how soon and in what manner the foreknowledge comes to sheep, that of all created beasts, their doom is sealed from the moment they are born. They are destined for one end, they come here only for that, and the bleating of a herd of them shows they know it, for of all melancholy, hopeless sounds, that is the saddest.

Of course, the doom of pigs is no less inevitable. Born to be eaten, they spend their days in preparation for that sacrifice, yet there seems to be a certain hardy intelligence in their species that saves them from the submissive sadness of the woolly animal. All smooth beasts are harder, more tempered and philosophical than the soft, hairy ones. Yet in all kinds, the black panther crouches, rides, swims, exults, and passes on.

The mares that have been hanging their heads for some time past and looking towards the earth, lie down now and push the foals out onto the meadow. Pensively they look around upon the wet, shining off-shoots of themselves and perhaps they wonder whence and whither, for going somewhere is the keynote to the being of horses, and all their life is a forward and back.

The young foal arrives with its delicate long legs in a

folded pattern, like a dark, unfurled flower; the sun makes it move and lengthen, rear its head and toss the curly mane until it is dry. How soon it braces its brand new forelegs and pushes itself up from behind! Then, searching out the milk by its sweet, necessary smell, it thrusts its little muzzle into the warm hollow and seizes the willing nipple, with no different instinct, eagerness, insistence and passion of gesture and need than of any lover for any love, and thirst of love and hunger anywhere on this earth where the black panther goes his way.

Now the air is full of white flakes, blowing easily sideways, not cold, as we knew them a while ago, but warm and carrying little lost apples. They are torn off the twigs in the orchards—the spring harvest, unfruitful of all but beauty. Autumn lingers behind, and in the denuded pistil patiently presses out the essence saved for a later bounty.

How the pigeons, circling in this gentle storm, beat through it and dip and rise again! Along the wall of the garden, their pink feet dig into warmed *adobe* as they pace to and fro, bowing, and beseeching of each other. Their perpetual drifts and rising shifts, with their ever-repeated drive and thrust into the cavity of reproduction. Their fire never goes out. It shines tenderly in the blue feathers, burning like rubies, and in the single spark of the eyes, set jewel-like in red tissue. The world is a soft flame that mounts higher, day by day, as the sun travels north and sets, now, nearer the northern Colorado ranges.

Towards evening the high, thin clouds are widened out into enormous billowing sails, roseate and warm above the dark hills. They do not hasten and hurry as in March. They are not driven as in April. This Maytime is becoming soft with a knowledgeable fullness of being—and soon this cup of earth will be running over.

In the Pueblo, the boys and young men give back power and speed to life. Issuing from the kivas with naked painted bodies, stuck over with eagle down, each one blows a feather to the sun. Then along the track that is hollowed by centuries of bare feet running this morning race in May and in September, they run in relays, putting forth every particle of energy they can summon up.

Teeth bared, heads back, they tear along the track lightly but with incredible swiftness, and they are giving back to earth and sun what they have received. In due time they will harvest it again, in wheat and corn, and fruit. The everlasting exchange goes on—between man and the earth, one and inseparable, but infinitely divisible.

The air, in the cold morning light, is full of a softer flood than flakes of snow or apple blossoms, for down from the breasts of eagles blows off the hair of flying boys, and off their swift limbs.

And when, at night, the moon shines over this valley, it illumines a soft, flaky movement of flowers and feathers and running water winding between white hedgerows and under lilac trees.

Often, in May, there is a faint-hearted sun that comes up over the eastern hills, shining wanly through thin, dusty clouds, when the bright blue is seen intermittently behind the floating rifts of shredded, tangled web. And soon it disappears and the round form is hidden altogether, leaving a white, opaque sky. The trees stand utterly still, as though listening all day long to the blinding glare of diffused light, and their young green seems to grow more vivid as the hours pass.

The leaves lose the sparkle they have when the sun turns each one into a little flashing mirror, flickering this way and that. They hang, mild and still, and the only movement in the branches comes from the birds, blue and gray and glistening orange and yellow, that hop busily back and forth, intent upon nests and eggs and young ones.

This kind of day passes like a dream wherein nothing happens. Far away on the side of a mountain sometimes a forest fire burns, and a column of smoke rises quietly like a specter against the black green solidity. The pensive sadness of such a day is like a cold, resigned hand upon one's forehead; everywhere the fire burns low.

But in the springtime no mood lasts long. In the afternoon, perhaps, off in the desert, rises a tall twister of yellow dust, whirling towards the town. Like a twisted column it stalks towards us, corkscrewing, sucking up into itself what it encounters upon its way—leaves, branches, old forlorn papers. Tony has told me that every one of these has a tiny animal in its center. I do not know what he means, but I have found that all he has said about other natural things has a fact behind it, so I wonder what germ, or insect, or cell of the wind is hidden in these folds. And I wonder, when I see them coming, if the Israelites were not led by such a column, moved across the desert by the prevailing wind towards the Promised Land.

The sky comes down dark and turns a thunderous black, and the apple trees are white against it and seem to support it. The dark sky between the white apple branches is one of the Maytime sights. The rooms in the house grow suddenly dim, and the green leaves against the windows filter in a livid, deep-sea light that is unnatural and makes one quail and move restlessly about, waiting for some culmination. Even the birds outside are still and seem to stop breathing. Then it comes.

The whole room is bright with an instantaneous white flash, and the crash of black clouds upon each other follows, the boom and breaking of gathered force. If one runs out into the garden, the apple trees seem to shine, incandescent, against the ominous thunder clouds; and now the animals have come out of their quietude: the birds are shrill with alarm, the horses are whinnying in the fields, and Tito stands barking on the bridge.

Does it mean rain is coming? Hardly, for Tony reminds me the flood is held up so long as the young birds are helpless in their nests. But a few drops fall, and as they slowly splash down, the sun breaks through over in the west and silvers every one, so that it is seen round and pear-shaped, glistening.

Soon the world shines all over, the leaves come alive and twist and turn, gleaming again, the flagstones are washed and sparkling darkly, and the sky draws up to an immeasurable height above the orchard where the apple trees shake themselves, glad to be free from the weight of it.

Perfume of lilacs and plum drifts across the late afternoon hours, and the pigeons wheel and drift off into it. Come! let's take a walk, let us move off into this fresh world, clear of the sulphur and the binding electric spell.

In the desert behind the house, every sagebush is washed clean and a heavenly smell comes out of the damp, assuaged earth. The rainbow embraces us. We are between its horns, that sprout, one in the Pueblo, and the other in Cañon. Walk and walk and walk, in the lovely lightened air, breathing deep, with a high heart.

And all this time, day after day, the fields are opening to the plow and the harrow. The Indians are busy in their earth, the Mexicans in theirs. Pushing open the furrows, loosening the tightened soil, men travel along the straight rows preparing the land for the seed.

On warm, sunny days, the Indians coil their white sheets around their heads like high turbans, or riding through the hedges, they shroud their faces in them. And happiness makes them sing like the birds in May, so that the land has an echo of song floating over it. Tony is away all day long, breaking his patches of land, getting some ready to sow with new alfalfa, some in wheat and oats.

The damp red earth clings to everyone's feet in May, and the floors of the house never stay clean. The field in front of the house, that only yesterday was dark and smooth, to-day is pricked through by an endless sea of sharp green blades. The oats are up! Max brings in the first mess of asparagus from the garden, and says we will eat our rhubarb tomorrow.

Now, on many days, the sky is pure blue and benevolent over the fields. The Sacred Mountain darkens where the deep color washes into the cedars, and the canyons open with a depth they had not while the cold congealed the earth.

And this of all the seasons of the year is the time when the world receives the light without the heat, when the fire is high and does not consume, when the energy in every atom holds itself in equilibrium, unspilled, unbroken, and trembling in its balance.

The high potentiality of Nature reaches its zenith, now, before the months of overflow, and everything shines in continence, holding its own. This is the splendor of the brimming cup, deep with poison and perfume, disastrous to those who will not pass it and leave it to ripen and mature. This is the profound reservoir where all the forces of life are gathered, and where the total dynamism of growth is present in every cell, and every cell has pooled its power to unite the diverse beauties of potency and promise.

Contemplate, adore, and withhold your hand from rifling the blossom; leave the flower to its own timely development; leave it to fall gently into fruition. Leave the nest unscathed, and the young birds to their gradual freedom to fly and escape from your appetites.

Yourself—recognize the spring light shining upon your

head, and do not miss the lovely moment of its withholden fire.

No other time in all the year will have this grace, this tempered ferocity, when all things pause, contained, before the inevitable, heavy plunge into the dense and solid harvest of these days.

And yourself, the vessel of the spring, you who need not be spilled if your balance holds, contrive to pass back to the needy universe this light before it thickens into heat and densifies in flesh, for here, my love, is where you may pass beyond the imperative of Nature and all adorable natural life, over beyond the rim of evolution and decay, to where the laws of corn and apples disappear, and true creation begins in high fecundity.

Sometimes in the early spring, one wakes to find the whole valley shrouded in gray clouds. I open my eyes upon the Sacred Mountain, and it is gone! A long, level bank of heavy grayness lies across it that reaches around the horizon as far as the eye can see. Sounds come to one muted through the mist, and the birds seem subdued. The horses out in the field stand as though they were hypnotized, their heads hanging. Everything looks a little drugged—and where has glad life gone?

The melancholy of spring descends upon one and it seems that nothing will ever be the same again. Life sinks down and one tries to account for the grayness in one's soul by blaming the letter that never came, or the burden of the income tax; but unless we eat or drink unwisely, no other thing is the cause of any mood from which we suffer than earth changes, and earthly imperatives.

I see Jose walking across the field taking Charley to the other pasture. Both of them walk as though their hearts were broken; there is no vitality in them. Under Jose's old Don Quixote hat, his face is hidden and his chin is on his breast. Charley follows languidly, lifting his feet as though each one weighs a ton. He raises his head a little and looks vaguely over towards the corral at Tony's House where Rosy stays at night, and he gives a low, feeble whinny, very basso and undone. Out of the deep stupor of spring there mounts in him a faint, premonitory hope that Rosy can bring life back to him again if he can only get near her. Oh, how sly of the ingenious spirit that governs our activities! To drop us down seven leagues before the new effort of fecundity must be made . . . *"reculer pour mieux sauter. . . ."* For this is the only way I can find to interpret the hopelessness of some spring days. They may be for us a measure of the ecstasy to come, "for there is no gainsaying it, Nature is essentially manic-depressive," I think, cleverly.

Tony comes up to my room after breakfast on a spring morning like this, and I roll my head listlessly towards him. I can feel the muscles in my face hanging down and I make no effort to be cheerful. Like the earth, I only know Now and forget it will ever be different.

Tony looks rather heavy himself, on such days. He sinks way down in himself and lets himself go as far as he feels like! Not with melancholy and not with *tristesse*, but with the slow, inevitable, unmoody weight of a large stone sinking into the ocean. His being seems to have departed, gone down into the depths, and when I say depths, of Tony, I mean depths! We others are shallow vessels compared with the profundity of his nature whose bottom I have never reached.

"Sad!" I comment, weakly, pointing one finger out the window.

"Natcherel," he replies, comfortably, letting himself down slowly into a chair. " 'Member that ring I showed you round the moon?" This, somehow, fails to console me. I just sigh to lift the weight off my breast.

"Goin' to rain, mebby," he continues. There is a contented look on his face as he gazes at the wall of cloud around us. Maybe he feels the same thing I do, without the name I give it. Sadness, melancholy, *tristesse*—these words condition us with their associations.

(*Il pleut sur la ville*
Comme il pleut dans mon cœur—
Now why should that be so mournful?)
Never mind! Let the pale smoke from our chimneys cling
to the ground, and the mist deepen on the hills; and do not
think in worldly terms of the birds' hushed singing. Nothing in nature is sad—that is only a word. But let us beware
of naming the day, lest we confine ourselves to the limitations of a language. If we are part of the color or tempo or
rhythm the world is in at any time, we are alive and there
is nothing of any greater significance than that, no matter
what the books say. . . .

I felt a little better, remembering what would come, and
I rang the buzzer.

Mrs. Gonzales mounted the stairs. She got the stove going and pulled the curtains and plugged in the little hot
water kettle for me, and in three minutes it was warm and,
living once more, I had my tea and felt better. It is strange
how the life dies down in rooms unless someone is constantly doing something to them.

Now the white ceiling was in shadow, except where the
golden light from the lampshades made queer shapes upon
it, and the big, white twisted columns had a yellow glow
over them.

The warmth brought out the smell of the freesias, and
the spreading light that hung in the center of the room came

down full upon a round, low pot of yellow tulips on the table, and seemed to draw them up to itself so that they reached and stretched and quivered, and one could almost see them grow and hear them living out their brief and vivid existence.

Down in the village at this hour, everyone was going in and out of the post office in the winter way.

Everyone was stamping the mud off their feet onto the post-office floor, and talking in little groups: Mexicans, Indians and Americans, Greeks, Assyrians and Germans, an Italian or two, a Russian or two, Scotch and Irish, and even a Portuguese, all citizens, of course, and all bent on getting letters and messages from somewhere else.

All day in their scattered houses and stores they have been rather slumbrous and still, for winter makes people quiet; but at the mail hour there is an exhilaration of consciousness and of sociability; they laugh and greet each other with smiles and good fellowship, clap each other on the back and crack a joke.

"Hello!" everyone says to everyone else, in energetic voices. When people pass each other on the road or in the Plaza at any hour of the day, they always greet one another with a nod and a "Hello," whether they are acquaintances or not. It's "Hello" all day long and all along the way; but it's a low, murmured word, a mere breath, just to show a pleasant feeling. In the post office, it's different; it's a brisk and cheery regular exchange, with usually a comment on the weather added: "Wonderful weather we're having?" Or, "Terrible, isn't it?"

The cars stop and start again out in the twilight. Two or three station wagons drive up from near-by ranches, and women in riding breeches and sheepskin coats pass in and out between men dressed just the same.

Everyone opens his or her box with a key or a combination of twirling arrows—except the long line of people whose mail comes to the General Delivery. The Postmaster of each new administration has to learn the patience his predecessor knew, for the same little old ladies timidly turn up their faces, night after night through the year, asking for the letter that never comes; the Indian boys are forever hopeful that their schoolmates from other reservations will remember to write as they promised they would; and there are usually a goodly number of children that just ask for the fun of it, not really expecting anything!

There is a good strong smell in the post office for an hour or so: *adobe* and overshoes and tobacco blended in cold. But go in there at six o'clock on a February night and the aroma has seeped away and it is like a quiet tomb, subdued and dim, with a solitary bulb throwing a vague light on the Postmaster's closed windows and on the rows and rows of mail boxes. People and animals, only, on this earth, can animate and stir the immobility of places, fill them with life and movement and a crackling vibration: when they are absent, inanimate objects droop and sag and lose significance.

When the last bit of twilight goes, two or three little Neon lights pop on in the Plaza over the two drug stores and in front of the hotel; and an occasional electric bulb, solitary as a star, suspended over a crossroad leading away.

Vegetable and fruit piled in MacMarr's window on one side of the courthouse, and Burch's and Beery's windows further along, show green and golden for a short time; but by six o'clock no one can go in and buy any more except on Saturday nights. So the Plaza empties gradually, and people are home in their houses eating supper.

On a stormy night like this, there are hardly any automobiles passing in and out of the village. A few stand parked in front of the court house and the drug stores, and the snow gathers on their hoods and tops, inches deep, and they look like huddled elephants in a row.

Ruth's Beauty Shop is at one side of Saavedra's drug store, and downstairs underneath it there is a Recreation Parlor. On such a night as this men will gather down there and play pool, and sit near the heater and swap stories.

Max brought the mail up to me before he went home,

and the bed was strewn with letters and papers and, happily, two new books from the Villagra Library.

Off in the outside world, Brett is somewhere in a room I don't know, talking with people I have never seen, painting a portrait I may never see. This seems strange to me, because we have been so much together for ten years and I am always able to visualize her in the places where she goes, for they have been familiar to me. Her letter had new, strange names in it and I felt as though she had got away from me!

Frieda, too, writing from far away, of curious new fruits and lovely embroideries, seemed to me away on another planet, for the winter isolation bore down on me this night and I couldn't overcome the sense of emptiness and silence that kept returning to confound me.

Supper was comforting, though. Hot cocoa and a chop and warm soda biscuits, crisp lettuce with a great deal of garlic flavoring the Italian oil, cheese and crackers, and a piece of cold pumpkin pie!

The Pooch strolled punctually up to my room when the tray came, smiling and groaning at the same time.

"Hello, Pooch," I said to her, but my voice sounded unnatural all alone by itself, as though I were making noises for their own sake. . . .

I wished there were more people about. If it were only springtime, the Penitentes would begin to go back and forth between the village and the *morada* behind the Big House.

This *morada* is built on a piece of Indian land leased for a long term from the Indians, and Tony's fence bounds the Calvary that stretches from the chapel to the great, hoary cross at the end that Georgia painted so often.

Every Friday night during Lent, the Penitentes congregate in the low building, called by the silvery bell in the little leaning belfry. As they pass the kennel where the Great Danes live, up against the main wall of our long house, the dogs thunder at them with deep, hollow barkings, and jump against the high wire. Up on top of a carved post, a flickering flame from the oil lamp, that Max lights every night in the year in the *placita*, throws mysterious shadows upon the high walls that surround it, and upon the bronze head of an Indian that Maurice made here seventeen years ago and gave to me, and that now rests upon a great cross-bar of ancient wood, bridging the two walls that enclose the garden of the St. Teresa House. The face seems to grin down sardonically in the fitful light, upon the dark shapes of men that creep up over the bridge and pass under the lamp on their way to their tryst.

The Indians have no emotional affiliation with the Penitente rites. They seem queer to them and unlike their own forms of worship, but at the same time they respect them. The Indians are the first to defend the Penitentes when some priest or politico tries to persecute them, and they are always welcome at the Pueblo Church.

Sometimes in the night, the singing voices wake me when they are marching up to the Calvary. There is a thud —thud that punctuates the wild anguish of the chant. All over the valley dogs wake and furiously bark; though people down in the village cannot hear this night chant, all the animals can. Horses turn and whinny nervously, and the barking of the dogs ends on a complaining whine.

When I get up and look out of the east window, I can see nothing, even if the moon is shining—only the small moving lantern one of them carries. They dip into a hollow and their voices diminish; then they emerge and the high agony is wafted over to me.

The land has been turned into a different place, the underworld rises and invades the darkness, and a spirit is abroad that has its habitation in the depths. They are letting it out, and it takes the desert for its own.

There is nothing even remotely Indian in the sound that comes across the sage and cedar to my ears; it is something that came from Spain, from the Moors, from Africa, perhaps.

The final celebration comes at the full of the moon, at the season that we call Holy Week. But how long before Christ walked this earth was this form conceived? All human utterance is an effort to crash the gate between consciousness and unconsciousness, to open a channel between the single sealed atom and the vast sea in which it exists, and to let a part of the undisclosed flow upwards to the outer racial life of air. All sound comes from another world, a world we cannot know but only dimly suspect; it is breathed forth and dies in the unfamiliar element: dying, it deposits its essence in our memories. Thus, little by little, we absorb and take into ourselves life from somewhere else; from somewhere so inconceivably remote to us that we have only negative names for it, like "the *un-*conscious." What we know is positive but useless to us once it is ours. We care nothing for the crystals of knowledge, but only for the flow of light—and we hanker for the experience of translation—for the moment when we are channels, bridges, mediums between the unformulated and the dead limitations of the Known.

So from the throats of singing Penitentes boils up a hot lava from an ancient magical incantation designed to loosen these streams.

In the spring, when there is a surging from within the earth, and many forces are moving, after the quietude of winter, strange thoughts rise in one while leaning from a window in the night. . . .

But when morning comes, after such a vigil, the world is shining and innocent of such intimations. The fields are so mild and calm, the sky so tender above them! I look out into the garden and smile to see the long fingers of the weeping willow so green where it sways in the gentle breeze. A sharp sound of hammering floats over to our house from somewhere in the neighborhood, for the carpenters get busy in the spring. Everyone repairs, or adds, or builds something.

Where is the strangeness of the night gone to in the morning?

Soon after Easter a troupe of men come along our ditch from Canon. That means the water will be running any day, now. Everyone, through whose property the ditch runs, must put on two or three Mexicans to help clean it of the rubbish and dead leaves that accumulate in the winter, or else pay for men to work. Max and Jose are always too busy so I pay the eight or ten dollars in fees.

The troupe of men come along, armed with picks and shovels, laughing and joking as they work. They are like a many-legged machine that eats up everything in its way. They dig and shovel the dirt out on either side of them, and sometimes it falls onto the tender plants that border the stream. They don't care. They just go on shoveling. They have axes with them, too, and sometimes they ruthlessly chop off branches of the elders or the cottonwoods that impede or narrow the flow, or they cut the willows back and leave the winding stream-bed bare and wounded-looking.

The *Major Domo* directs them, looking only to the good of the ditch. The importance of water is nowhere greater than here, and upon this old irrigation system, laid out who knows how many hundreds of years ago by the Indians, depend the crops for the coming year—all the wheat and corn, the vegetable gardens, the alfalfa and hay. Is it any wonder they look more to the depth and breadth of the channel than to the pretty flowers along its borders? I believe they resent the water going to flowers in the summer-time, even if one has paid the peons for one's share in the up-keep and has the right to the water for whatever use one will put it to. Water means food to these men—to others of us it means sweet peas and roses as well as oats, peas, beans and barley. . . .

Then, one morning, one wakes up to hear the water rushing and bubbling below the window! How lovely! After the tight frozen winter and the dusty winds of spring, to hear the water flow again! It has come all the way from Blue Lake, up in the mountains behind the Sacred Mountain; it has fallen six thousand feet through canyons where its sides were bordered with pine and aspen trees; it has come down through the scrub oak and the mountain elders, until it reached the Pueblo. Then it has run over stones in a broad stream where the cottonwoods hang over it and suck it into their roots so that they grow a yard every year.

The Indians have charge of the water for three miles downwards to the town, then a Mexican takes charge of it. The Ditch Boss is supposed to ride the ditch every day from the time it is turned on until the day it is turned off in the fall. Fourteen miles of ditch to superintend daily, to see that the water is used fairly by each in turn, and that no one steals from another.

But Lee was the man who seemed to me to do this job the best. I used to see him, gaunt and red-headed, riding his mare with one arm, for he had lost the other in his saw-mill. All summer long the intricate ingenious arrangement of head-gates, side-streams and divisions make it possible for everyone to have water by turn, unless there is a drought, and then it is very painful indeed.

It is possible to see the leaves uncurl themselves when the ditch runs. They unroll, and soon all the trees are a bright, shrill green. The wild plum trees that border it above here, and that bound the fields that are getting water now, burst suddenly like popcorn into their white flower. Then the whole valley is perfumed with them; one brings branches into the house and sets them in jars of water, and the smell penetrates into every corner: the loveliest flower-scent in the world, I think. But one thinks that at every step of the year, when the other flowers come along! Still, there is something particularly poignant and wonderful about the fragrance of the plums.

Everything moves so suddenly in the spring. The sun will be shining some sweet afternoon, and in an hour the cloud full of rain rolls over the mountain. It turns to hail and comes down in white lines of ice, threatening the young shoots in the field. All of a sudden it ceases, and one end of a thick, bright rainbow sprouts right out of the Pueblo. I can see it from my room, and I run to the eastern window and find the other end stuck in the hillside behind the house. The perfect arch shimmers in beatitude, all smiling and sparkling. Once Tony was there, and I cried:

"Oh, look! There is the end of it behind the house!"

He looked, but as he looked, he said, correcting me: "*Indians* never point at the rainbow."

"Oh, why, Tony? Why?" I begged.

"That's enough," he answered, firmly, shutting me up. . . .

I wished Tony would come back. I had been trying not to think about that ever since it grew dark, but I had been feeling it just the same. The storm frightened me as it had a thousand times before, the continuity of the softly falling, silent snow. It reminded me of a picture in a book I had when I was a child, called "Prince Peerless." The picture was labeled, "The Snow Woman," and she stood tall and white and absolutely motionless, her eyes lowered while the snow fell and fell about her.

To change these thoughts I tried again to go back into spring, summer, autumn, and remember what I loved in them, but somehow these seasons seemed to have their own terrors in the beauty and I recalled what happened to Tito and poor Kitty and Thyla and Donska too.

One day when I came in from riding, I heard a faint, far-away crying and moaning as I walked through the garden, but the trees shut out the sound, making a hushed enclosure that nothing penetrates distinctly, and it was impossible to distinguish what it was or where it came from. When I was down, after changing my clothes, I heard it once more, nearer, over by the *acequia*, a heart-broken sobbing, every breath a low cry of pain.

"What is that?" I thought, my attention caught by something familiar in it. "What is that, Max?" I asked, seeing him come across the little bridge over the *acequia*.

"Well, our neighbor shot Tito," he said. "I think he has crawled under here," he added, bending down to look.

"Tito!" He had started out with us that morning, so sprightly and chipper, frisking along in the sunshine, leaping up like a rabbit to look over the sagebushes, every hair on fire with electricity, happy little Tito! He must have turned back before we did.

"Who shot him? Montano?" I cried. He lives behind Tony's house on the other side of the ditch.

"Yes. Tito was digging in his vegetable bed and he shot him," stated Max.

"Get him out from there and bring him up to the house," I ordered. "Is he hurt much?"

"No, I don't think so. I guess he's just shot in the leg."

He reached in under the platform with a long wire and hooked him out, and I could hardly bear the sounds; when he carried the limp soft little thing into the house there was a trail of blood behind him. We laid him on a rug in the east plant room where he and Pooch slept every night and I knelt down beside him and put my hand on his head.

"Oh, Tito! Why did he have to do that?"

He was breathing in a rapid, sobbing way, and moaning with every breath, and the sound seemed to say, "Why did he do that? It hurts so—it hurts so," and he turned his head and tried to reach my eyes to ask me: "Why? Why? Why did he do that?"

Was he only shot through the leg? I turned it over to see and the blood was welling up from the hole that went right through his belly and was forming a pool under him. His little body was shrinking while I watched him. I just couldn't bear it. I got up and left blindly and he raised his voice louder to call me back, so I went. He had lifted himself up and was wavering from side to side on his feet and the blood trickling down.

"Oh, Tito—lie down—lie down—" but no, he seemed to gather himself together and he slowly and carefully walked past me, making a clear little imprint of blood on the floor with each foot as he did so. He made his way to the door of the first bedroom and stood there waiting for me to open it. He seemed to know so well what he wanted that I had to do what he wished.

I opened the door and he walked stiffly and slowly across the floor, and already he was attenuated like a dim yellow wraith, and on every rug there were those bloody footprints. He came to the next closed door, the one that leads into Tony's room, and when that was opened, he made his way over to the bed and stood beside it. He looked up at me. "Put me up there," he seemed to be saying. "I want to die up there on Tony's bed."

I only knew then that it was really fatal, for he told me so, in that way. . . .

Max came in after me and carried him back to the sun room. Then Ledibor came in and I asked him to look at Tito. I waited in the book room while he did so but it was no use. I knew that. He came back to me and said: "Not a chance, Mabel. He's bleeding to death. He is suffering very much."

"End it, then," I cried, and rushed upstairs, weeping. I lay on the bed and under the window I heard the men's voices. I thought I should have gone with Tito while Ledibor did it but I could not. Then I heard the shot. What a waste! What a waste! It all seemed so unnecessary.

When Tony came in I told him.

"Tito is dead," I said, and I related all about it and how he wanted to die on his bed.

His eyes filled with tears. "He was our friend," he said. "I always liked him just the same, though I pretended." Then he went out to see Montano.

I went out riding again late that afternoon with Myron, and because he saw the tears running down my face as we rode, the other dogs bounding along so joyously, and Tito just blotted out, he said:

"There was something fitting about his end—that violence—there was always a wildness about him—"

That night Tony and I came in the gate in the moonlight and only Pooch ran out to meet us. Tony said, "Poor Tito. We are going to miss him a long time—always bringing you a present—"

If the white plum blossom was the sign of spring along the hedges and between the fields, the wild sweet briar rose is the early summer flower. It comes shyly at first but soon it is a pink froth all over the bushes that are thick in the lanes. The little wide-open single roses have a deep sweet perfume and there is something so romantic about this fragrance that one softens and grows dreamy under its influence. It is the odor of June, of tender nights and mild soft days. The young Indian girls go out and gather the rose petals and dry them, then they spread them among their clothes. Married women strew them between the clean clothes they have washed for their husbands so they leave a little perfume behind them when they pass. All the women roll them between finger and thumb into little hard beads and string them into sweet chains they wear under their dresses. June is always fragrant, with the wild roses perpetually near, indoors and out, in the warm folds of cotton, and all along the paths we have to go.

The trees grow dark and heavy, so thick their foliage, so unbrageous, they form an impassable wall at the west along the *acequia madre*, shutting out the sounds of the village and keeping the evening breezes off the house. Only from the open eastward side of the house where there are no trees, comes the cooling night air down from the Pueblo Canyon, and I move my bed from the north end of the room where it looked out on the mountain all through the winter and spring, but which has a screen of silver leaves before it now, over to the alcove where the casement win-

SPRING EVENING (*photograph by Edward Weston*)

GOING FISHING

dows let in fresh winds all night long, winds scented with drenched sagebrush after the afternoon rain, and cedar whipped by summer hail, and the hot dust of noon that has given way to the pungent scent of wet desert earth.

Four willow trees stand at the corners of the platform over the *acequia madre*. Their long, thin branches turn over from the tops of each of them and hang to the ground swaying like women's hair turned over to dry in the sun. One must part the yellow-green and shining supple strands and pass between them to go out to the swings. There is a shade all around one out here, with sunlight filtering through it. A round, cool cavity in a thick meshwork of many green tones. Locust, willow, cottonwood, wild plum, silver beach, and mountain elder, all these are intertwined and make a transparent tapestry. Outside this retreat, between the *acequia* and the house, the hollyhocks have sown themselves so thick between the flagstones they make a pink and red forest that one must wind in and out of. They hide the house, and from the house they hide the whole courtyard and the big front gate. There are hundreds of them, six and seven feet tall, swaying and bending in the sunshine, dripping in the rain, always alive with the bronze and blue humming birds. The pigeons waddle in and about their shadowy feet where among yellowed fallen leaves and damp, cool stalks there are myriads of odd tidbits, snails and slugs and earthworms.

The wild olive tree against the south window of the Rainbow Room has grown huge and billowy and its branches are flattened against the glass and its tip passes above the roof. This and the locust by the west window shade the room, dimming it down to twilight and an evening gloaming.

All the lower rooms of the house are darkened in the summertime by the encroaching trees, except in the morning when the sun comes in the east windows.

My big room upstairs is dim too from the drawn curtains of pale yellow and green silk, when my breakfast tray comes up to me at half-past seven. The corners are gray and there is a quietude and peace in the cool shadows. At this hour down town in the Plaza, the energetic tourists are strolling about early, poking their noses into the windows of curio shops, pointing out the picturesque characters among the Mexicans and Indians, or the cowboys in their big hats who ride into town looking for a dude to take out on horseback. These tourists are dressed with the indifference of appearance of those who sacrifice vanity to convenience in places where they will only see people they will never see again.

The women are usually fitted out in long trousers or beach pajamas, and either boudoir caps or large hayfield straw hats. Frequently they wear glasses and wrinkle their noses in the bright sunshine. The men are in their shirt sleeves with odd suspenders over their shoulders, and they carry coats on their arms. Their shapes are formed by sedentary occupations and they seem to miss their accustomed routine as they wander aimlessly about behind their women.

The Plaza is lined with cars with licenses from Colorado, Texas, and Oklahoma, with an occasional one from New York or New England and there is always a slow, perpetual movement in the dusty square from those who hopefully look for a parking place. All day long they drive to the Pueblo and sign the book in the Governor's house, and are herded about by one of the Indian officers of whom they ask ten thousand foolish questions: "Do Indians really go to church? Do Indians eat vegetables? Why don't they dance more in July and August when so many people come here?" The guides answer patiently, only their eyes betraying their amusement.

I hardly ever go down to the Plaza in the summer. Up here on the hill there are so many pleasant places to hide away in, cool, shady, quiet, of what use to become irritated by the slack crowded atmosphere of the village, invaded as it is by the vacant-eyed tourist population?

Down in the orchard the old apple trees spread wide low branches and in the open space where they grew too old to bear any more, the rows of peas, beans, cauliflower, carrots, beets, squash, and many more besides, are heavy with fresh new vegetables. The corn has followed the daily green peas, as they succeeded the asparagus. The cherry tree has borne its fruit and now we have rows of canned cherries on the pantry shelves ready for pies and tarts. The green gages are bursting and their sweet syrup runs over onto the ground. We can sit in the dark shade beneath the trees and eat the warm plums and read the August magazines, and forget the village.

In the summer, over in the St. Teresa garden down the line from the Big House, there are two hammocks strung between the trees, and wicker chairs upon the grass. Behind the garden wall, behind the long sienna-colored curtains that hang upon the old crossbeam between the *adobe* walls, there is the somnolence of summer afternoons with the sound of bees and locusts in the air, and the freshness that comes wafted across from the sprinkler. The leaves overhead flicker a little to let the sunlight sparkle through, and occasionally a sweet August apple drops to the ground, with a small thump. In the morning our friends there think it is pleasant to drink coffee and eat eggs and bacon, marmalade and hot toast on the old table under the trees and look away below the branches across the curving *acequia* and see the desert swimming in a blue haze, see across the miles of jade green stretches to the narrow opening out of the Rio Grande Canyon, where the highway comes up from Santa Fe; in the evening to lie in the hammock and watch the moon circle through the high branches of the cottonwood tree, its leaves motionless and black as thin iron.

The dogs we like so well lie at our feet, each near the one loved best, and from the house we can hear the radio playing, with the seductiveness that distance imparts to it, the soft, muzzy melodies of modern dance music.

The grass is cool under one's fingers in the night, and lying on a serape one can comb the soft crisp blades; talk is intermittent and unfocused in such hours, unlike the brisk argument and the sharp rejoinder of electric-lighted rooms; and time slides by unheeded, sleepily, and perhaps a little sadly, perhaps a little wistfully, with a tinge of undefined desire, the night is so beautiful, so fair, and unpartaken. It seems then to one that Nature provides sometimes a beauty to which we are unequal, and that we are seemingly without the gesture and response that would adequately fit the scene. Paralyzed, we faintly realize that we are ourselves only the tourists in the Garden of Eden! How ever recover again the true relationship and intimacy with beauty, so we are no longer mere outsiders?

Twelve o'clock comes, and the moon is high and bright in a clearing of the sky, and we rouse ourselves to say

good-night and go out of the garden and home across the
open *placita* where the old Spanish lantern burns on a
carved post in the center of empty space. The moon shines
brightly on part of the walls and the pilasters are black
in the shadow. Over the gate in an archway of *adobe* hangs
the old bronze chapel bell. The black and pale shades of
moonlight and shadow on all the walls and buildings here
make them look like some fabulous setting by Gordon
Craig or Robert Edmond Jones, for a play without an ending, for there is a curious enchantment brooding over this
odd, empty, open space. It is partly bounded by the high
walls of the Big House courtyard and the garden walls of
St. Teresa. The east side is backed by the small house with
the pink portal and it is outlined against the black foothills
behind it; an old Penitente lodge has been fashioned into
one of the garages with the great Danes' pen behind it; the
long, low, carpenter shop on the west side with its spindled
windows has long, black, cottonwood branches hanging
over it, and the opening in all this enclosure comes at the
bridge across the *acequia*, where one plunges down the hill
and away from here on those rare occasions when one
must. The trees meet overhead and the bridge is the dark
floor of an exit through green leaves flanked by two massive *adobe* pillars. On the outside of one is fastened a small
blue panel where silver letters say: "Private Property. No
Admittance. Tourists Unwelcome." But even so, too often

in the daytime cars rush up the hill and circle the central carved post with its leaning lamp, and the round seat at its base. They move around once with craning heads and pointing fingers, and twice, unless someone meets them with a cold eye and an enquiry about their business, whereupon they look apologetic and silently speed away. What, one wonders, do they conjure up of fascination and mystery in the life beyond the two pairs of heavy carved gates leading into the St. Teresa House and into the Big House? The acacia tree hangs over the wall, the golden cock, upon the housetop back beyond the silver beeches and the wild olives, gleams and turns in the sunshine and in moonlight; the house itself is embedded in foliage; no sound comes from inside except the faraway, fantastic cries of the parrots and all is silent, unseen, and full of portent. So it must appear to the Texans and the Oklahomans who reach the outer edge of this oasis. So it appears to us, as a matter of fact, who live at the center of its strange, adorable enclosure and are unable at times to fully realize and appreciate the magic of an environment created by ourselves.

Now the canyons are deep in shade and after the humming heat in the long, flat desert sagebrush, it is a relief to plod slowly up the mountain on the sweaty horse and feel the cool air on one's face.

Every once in a while the path emerges onto the open slope high up, cut across the stony earth, horizontal, with the wide valley swimming below, gray and blue and patched with yellow, where the wheat and oats are ripening.

Now one sees one's world laid out down there—a world that is sufficient in its variety, a world of change and subtlety, forever elusive, rich in its beauty and danger. The Pueblo is two low hills of brown earth pyramidal on either side of the creek, and it lies at the foot of the huge mountains whose crest is shaped like a bow. There is no flash or flicker from these earthy piles, for no glass veils any but the church windows, but blue piñon smoke hovers over them from dozens of squat chimneys.

The long cottonwood edging of the river winds down to the town and these trees that are a film of gray lace in winter are heavy and dark now, and seem like solid green humps, and as the English landscape painters would have seen them.

One knows that if one were down there, one would meet singing Indian boys, riding under the trees with wreaths of green leaves bound around their heads, and in those faraway fields others are working under the sun with the white sheet wound round and round above the faces, burned darker in the summer sunshine.

One morning, we rode up the canyon between the mountains southeast of the Pueblo. Tito and Pooch, Thyla and Donska were along, Tito always in the lead, darting like a streak of red fire, his ears pointed, Pooch far in the rear, with her ears laid back, streamline against her black bullet head, and the two Danes winding in and out of the pine trees and the underbrush with their noses to the ground.

We went up, up, up, very slowly on our plodding horses, for it was steep and Charley would stop every once in a while, brace his hind legs and heave a sigh and stretch out his head, but Nelly, in front, would keep going. Without any pleasure in life, a snarl of tangled hair over her face, she would watch the rear from the corner of her eye. She is the most sagacious mare in the world, well behaved and obedient, fast and strong, but utterly without the joy of life. Her back is deep and upholstered like a rocking chair, her rhythm is even, and she has a smug, swinging gait that never tires one, but she hasn't a particle of excitement in her, no electricity, no emotion. On and on she goes, the leader of them all, her only personal wish being that she must be first. She cannot endure being behind any other horse, so she never slackens or relaxes, like Charley and the others do, but keeps going evenly, endlessly, up and down these mountains, or across these desert roads.

The morning I am telling about she led the way up the trail with that untiring, deliberate gait of hers, and the dogs wove in and out between the legs of the horses and the trees. It was like a dream that goes on and on and will never end. We did not talk, but lost ourselves in reverie, half noticing now and then the flowers that were in bloom, the flaming Indian paintbrush, the garlands of wild wisteria that were thrown across the bordering trees, and the sweet chokecherry blossoms. There were fresh cobwebs glimmering between the branches and these we rode across and broke, and the earth had the deep, dark wet odor of rain that had fallen before sunrise. All this one noticed half unconsciously, just as one was always breaking off the young, new, tender tips of the pine twigs and eating them, or breaking off the hard old needles to chew, hardly knowing it. It was an hour of the most perfect ease and pleasure without thought or care, high up in the mountain in the fresh, early morning.

We came to the round level space that has no egress, that should have a trail leading up out of it and over the crest, but that apparently has not, but is walled with steep, thick mountain sides planted close with bushes and low scrub oaks, and those woven in and out with briars and barberry and other bristling things.

Pooch threw herself on the bed of pine needles that waited in the shade. She gave a jerk like an extenuated sausage, and keeled over in the relief of resting for a while, but the other dogs were out of sight, some distance away, nosing around and as we leaned forward on our horses to rest our backs, we heard them baying over beyond. The sweat steamed up from the horses and the cool mountain breeze dried the moisture on our faces and everything was all smooth and quiet.

Then all of a sudden, horror! I heard quick breathing and a scuffling in the dried leaves beside me and looking down I screamed: "Thyla!" The sight of her was an unbearable agony, and at the same time it had a look of crazy fun about it, filling one with sudden hysterical laughter. Her whole face, her nose, her tongue were bristling with white porcupine quills, her muzzle was a round ball, nightmarish like a Chinese grotesque, and her yellow eyes gleamed and showed the whites. Braced up on her hind legs she rubbed her head on the ground and she tried to rub her face with her paws, only to drive the hooked ends further into the flesh, and break them there, releasing the poison. She writhed and twisted, panting, and white foam ran out of her mouth. I saw Donska with her tail between her legs beat it down the trail. Just seeing her mother flayed with the backslamming defense that sews hundreds of sharp quills into flesh with one whack, had horrified her and galvanized her into flight, and she never would go up that trail again, but always left us at the foot of it and turned back home.

Calling Thyla, urging her along, we kicked our horses alive and galloped down the steep trail. Stumbling, pelting our way down, with the flying hooves starting stones bounding down with us, helter-skelter, we galloped as fast as we could and the tortured dog came as well as she could, too; but she was forced to stop every moment or two, trying to rub her burning pain out on the damp earth, but only making it worse.

One could not help participating in that agony, feel the close ruthless intensity of pain that had suddenly astonished the sensitive flesh of the cheeks and the tongue and the flickering nostrils, and share the horror of the forest that in one flash bristled from her long, lean head. How we galloped! Anything to bring that misery to an end, any risk to ourselves and the horses was nothing in the need to wipe out that impossible and perverted picture that, however, was printed on our memory forever like a shameful, unforgettable monstrosity. The distance that had taken us two hours to accomplish was covered in that downward flight in thirty-five minutes—and at home again we got the dog into Max's hands and Jose, having tied her legs together, began the long, slow task of drawing each quill out with a pair of pliers. Her head was covered with blood and foam, every pointed arrow was barbed at the tip, and they were embedded and hooked in the swollen flesh so that it was impossible to loosen them, except with a quick, tearing pull that ripped through, leaving dozens of minute slashes. Thyla was marvelous. She lay like a stoic and moaned when she could not suppress herself, but she made no attempt to struggle. She rolled up her long eyes and beseeched me to do something. I went into the house, not able to do anything and not able to watch the thing through.

Pooch arrived at the back door an hour later, covered with dust, her eyes staring, red-rimmed, out of the pale mask that was like a clown's. Her tongue hung four inches of dripping red from her mouth, her scalloped cheeks were drawn back in a mirthless grin and she gave me one disillusioned glance as she staggered down to the ditch for a drink.

She looked as though, if she could talk, she would say: "Well, *really—!*"

There are trees planted near the house below each of the waterspouts that lead the rain off the roofs down onto the ground, and these trees have grown rapidly from all the moisture they have soaked up, so in the summer we are buried in green darkness, and the *adobe* is almost hidden on the west side of the house where the long portal runs past the bedrooms.

On the east side facing the mountains and the desert, there are no trees and the windows are wide open to the sun. Out here there is a great regimented overflow of iris plants, the ones we have thinned out from the borders. They stand in rows, like an army waiting to be moved, but there is hardly any more space left to transplant them into, for there are iris flowers blooming everywhere in May, all along the ditch, the paths, around the trees, in every garden on the hill.

There is this curious contrast between the two sides of the house, where the back of it is so bare and exposed and runs along endlessly, like a train with a locomotive at one end of it, powdery dry with a crumbling soft surface, baking forever in the hot sun, lashed by the rain and snow, strung with countless wires in the crude methods of this neighborhood, telephone wires, electric light and power wires, radio wires, festooned and swinging carelessly, and every window drinking in the light, blankly unshaded, facing the glare.

But on the west side of the house there is the deep protection, the dark umbrageous quietude of summer, where thick, soft green leaves endlessly padding row upon row, making the hush and somnolence lie against the windows and the walls, and create a perpetual shade in the rooms.

Look inside the great gates that swing in the high *adobe* walls, separating this enclosure where the house is standing over there, smothered in flowers and green branches, and all that can be seen of it is the black, shadowed space between the posts of the portal, that marks the long, cool passageway where chairs and benches stand under the roof. In front of it, lumps of solid green, are round masses of trees, thickly leafed and healthy, shutting in the house.

The wild olive, pale gray green upon the light *tierra amarilla* wall, brushes against the window of the Rainbow Room. In June, the bittersweet perfume fills the air around the garden and penetrates into every chamber and then the heavy clusters of flowers are transformed into tiny, shrunken simulacra of olives, pale and sterile seeming, but some of the birds like them, and they are forever in and out of the long branches that bend over and touch the ground.

The round bed of flowers in the center of the flagstone space is rimmed by a little fence. Inside it, the pink and yellow hollyhocks stretch up, trying to outreach each other, the sweet nicotina flowers open in the evening here, and there is an odd tangle of other blossoms, purple petunias, bleeding hearts and lavender stock. Outside the jutting log cabin there is an acacia tree that grows larger every

165

year. It stands in the grassy lawn that is between the *patio* and the flagstone space, and all its branches curve over with the weight of its white clusters of bloom, and when these are finished they are replaced with long, hard, dry pods, curving in brown, comb-shaped, brittle cases where the seeds lie. Summer is dizzy with the perfumes of these trees and flowers, and there is a high humming that fills the house with sleepy music from the bees and cicadas, and the invisible, small insects that are everywhere, but scarcely ever seen.

These, too, have their odors and their menace. There is the black beetle that gets stepped on and fills the air with a sharp, sour smell that comes into the room on one's shoes and gets rubbed into a rug, so that it lingers sickeningly for hours. Spiders multiply prodigiously. They fight their way into the house through the cracks in the screens, they run over the floor, across the silk cushions, and up and down the long threads that hang before one's eyes.

Everyone fears the deadly "Black Widow," the poisonous one whose bite is fatal. We all know her and watch out for her. She had two red bands crisscrossed on her belly and long bowed arms; and we all fear the red ants too, that poison one with their bite, though not fatally. The ground is alive with ants of all kinds perpetually through the summer and fall, and the fields are thick with grasshoppers that rise in a green spray before one as one crosses through them.

All the rooms are cool and sound is muffled in them by the leaves against the open screened windows. One lies on the couch after lunch and reads, and the organdie ruffles on dresses grow crushed and damp and little wafts of perfume rise from here and there.

When afternoon grows late, it is nice to go out under the trees along the ditch, and have tea and iced drinks upon the platform that hangs over the water, and to lie in the swings there and look up into the intricate pattern of branches that makes a green roof over one.

Up there the locust and the willow, the maple, the elm and the cottonwood are all woven together. Lower down, the wild plum bushes reach up and tangle themselves with the others, and along the banks of the stream, long spongy leaves and water plants hang over the water.

There is a vivid light here under the trees where the sun comes darting through intermittently but it is of a darksome vividness, very rich and somber. The willow branches hang over the entrances to this retreat and the hollyhocks make a wall between it and the outer world so one is safe, concealed from anyone approaching the house. The sun begins to lower across the fields that one is looking down on from this lovely bank, and on the other side of them I know the little houses stand, but they too are buried in trees and not to be seen. The Pink House is lost behind the massy plum bushes and the others are engulfed in the green. Our voices are a little stifled by all this vegetation that is breathing about us, and our thoughts are not as keen as in other seasons. One becomes submerged, drowned in the flaccid luxury of summer.

When the sun sinks behind the trees over in the west, the air grows suddenly cool, and dozens of small birds start chirping overhead in the dusky dome of branches; they dart to and fro seeking the place to sleep, and the air is full of sound. It is chilly and one must rise and gather up pillows and books and bags, and go into the house once more.

It is strange how one comes slowly to realize that under the velvety thick curtain of summer leaves, when one lives hidden beneath the drowsy hush and fragrance deep in garden gloom, it is then of all the days in the year that violence and tragedy are nearest one, that then of all times one must be on the alert, wary, ready to dodge the blow and avert the falling fate. Perhaps it is because the whole circumambient air is permeated and possessed by the fierce mothers who are all on the *qui vive* to protect their young. So Thyla, nosing under the dark bushes, coming upon the baby porcupines, must be lashed by the flail that sews the stinging quills into her muzzle, so she turns tail and runs for dear life, and the young ones are saved.

It is on summer evenings that Tony will come home with a long face and say,

"Bad news. One of the mares kick a boy in the head."

One sees instantly the little foal by its mother's side, furry and fuzzy, the boy coming too near, and the quick flash of the hoof upraised and striking. So it is in summer that we lose our animals, and it is in the most peaceful days that the worst things happen.

But that is the way it is in these months. It is the same with fires. They break out on summer nights, the fire siren wakens us all with its weird rising wail in the silence; one looks out the window and there is a red glare beating up and down in the sky.

Everyone dresses hastily and rushes to town to help extinguish it, but there is no water save in wells and the bucket brigade cannot conquer the flames that are soon soaring. How livid and unfamiliar the faces of people look in the pinched green dawn when it comes!

What heat forces are commanding the summertime? The solar power, the blood heat, all the fires are loosened! In August the electrical storms waver and shimmer over the mountains and the air is full of unspeakable tension, on summer nights. The yellow leaves picture the conflagration that was endured, for later on, in September, when the aspen forests are painted yellow splashes upon the high slopes, their color seems to show what a passion burned through them to reach this culmination which is like the fires that blazed on summer nights.

Fire and color of fire blaze through the summer wild flowers. Masses of goldenrod bloom along the banks of the *acequia madre,* and in the fields the bright Indian paintbrush makes one think of sudden tongues of flame darting out of the surrounding green. Little green leaves growing up the stalk flush first with pink and go on to rosier warmth until the tip is a fiery vermilion. Sometimes when one goes up a hill one sees above one a clump of these scarlet blossoms swaying against the deep blue sky like beacon fires and it is a shock to the senses and the marvel of it is difficult to take in.

Fiery color washes through everything and surges up into all the fruits. Along the four narrow lanes between our house and the Pueblo, the thick wild plum bushes are laden with hard balls that hurry into ripeness and maturity; from palest pink to mauve, they deepen rapidly day by day to red and crimson, to every shade of warmth. Riding through these rich shady alleys one can smell the sweetness of the fruit, but bite into one, and it is sour and acrid yet, needing weeks more of summer heat to go pouring through.

Color deepens on the birds and the red flash of the woodpecker across the sky is like the quick red blossom of a flower, as the wild canaries, flitting among the green leaves, are like slick yellow lilies given to flight.

The field below the house is waist high now with oats, and long processions of slim, elegant turkeys mince in and out of the stalks, calling to each other, piping with high, thin, dreamy notes that finally get on one's nerves. This goes on monotonously for hours and then it suddenly breaks into a shrill chorus of panicky squawks, and the flapping of wings, for Mary and Phillip, the two wicked new Spaniels, have escaped from the kitchen and are leaping in and out of the oats in pursuit of them.

Mary and Phillip came to live here unexpectedly. They were unlooked-for guests and at first unwelcome ones, for two more undisciplined animals I never saw. Pale gold wigwags they are, all tumbled curls and soft brown eyes, ears full of burrs, and the long feathers around their large soft feet are a tangle and a misery. But Mary, with her wide-open look, resembles Greta Garbo, and Phillip is the image of Gary Cooper, and gradually they have won our hearts. But all they live for is to chase birds, it being bred in them to do so, and it is either turkey panic or pigeon fluster, or chicken horror all day unless they are shut up.

The corn is ripening on the stalks while the oats condense their substance, and the vegetables sprawl in uneven rows through the orchard, pumpkins, and squash swelling and burgeoning; onions, beets, carrots and cucumbers are so luxuriant one cannot make use of them all, even though from all the little houses the different maids go gathering for their families. There is always someone picking beans or gathering summer apples, or feeling out a pumpkin down in the orchard. Summer dresses flash behind the long low apple branches, and in and out of the corn, pink, and blue and lavender.

The asparagus is finished and has been cut down. The peas are over and only the vines left in a dry tangle for the little pigs to nozzle in.—The little pigs that were born soon after their sire ruined our horses, and now in a few weeks' time are themselves small fat replicas of him. They are supposed to be penned up but they, too, escape; no slit is too small for them to wiggle through, and if there is no opening, they burrow. They are here, there, everywhere, small ruddy atoms, scampering like mad, curly tails flying and hind legs tossed high. They have an almost insane intelligence in their glancing eyes, as they go pelting past one in exultant escape, but just call: "Piggy, piggy, piggy," and they cannot help but come.

Like the leaves and flowers and birds that appear and have their brief existence and are no more, and are perpetually succeeded by others, so it is with everything we know. The relentless succession goes on and nothing can stop it.

When the pressure of the solar energy makes us nervous and restless sometimes in the summer months, so it does to our little animals, too. One August afternoon I had crept into the darkest corner of the Big Room, after drawing the curtains over the east windows, and I had closed the front door so that not a slash of light could get into the room. There on the couch I lay and thought: "It seems to me I can't stand another hour of sunshine!"

Though it was dusky in the long room, and the silence was thick, and every movement of my starched muslins sounded muffled and cool, so one ought to have been able to forget summer, yet one had the consciousness of that great, flaming ball outside there, bending down upon the world like a god who comes too near and appalls by his radiance, and sears with his glory, burning up living things by a smile. I could still feel the thick blast of sunlight that was pouring down upon the valley, upon the fields, turning them to yellow hour by hour, upon the motionless trees that seemed to thicken and bend and grow dark under the weight of golden light. I knew the horses and cows would have sought out black shadowy spots to hide away in, the back of the barn, the back of the shed, behind the straw pile, around any corner, under any tree, and the chickens would be standing still, moody and broody, one leg drawn up, waiting for evening; the turkeys, weaving in and out of the deep shadows at the bottom of the oat field would still be peering and dipping as they hunted slugs and bugs, and out on the lawn with the sprinkler cooling the air under the acacia tree, there would be the blue and white pigeons snuggling down into the short wet grass, spreading their wings to catch the fine drops, cooing and gurgling, and maybe only they of everything alive on this hill were really comfortable.

The dining room door opened and Albidia's dark head came around into view and she was smiling and excited. She said:

"Kitty's acting very funny. We think she's sick."

"Oh, where?" I asked plaintively. I didn't want to cope.

"Out here behind the house."

I got up, and, smoothing my hair down and shaking out my crumpled skirts, I followed her through the kitchen and the back door to the desert.

There, in the vast open place where the heat wavered up from the sagebrush and made the mountains over eastward seem to be writhing, Kitty crouched against the *adobe* wall and gazed with eyes of horror upon something we could not see. The maids stood together twisting their aprons over their heads and giggling. The mere reflection in those dilated eyes of what that cat confronted in the landscape, the monstrous Beyond-Reality that one knew she had pressed out to penetrate, something hidden forever from us all but by some accident attained to by our Kitty, was embarrassing those girls. They stared at her, and Kitty stared at nothingness.

"Poor Kitty! Poor Kitty!" I murmured with tender inadequacy in the face of the immeasurable and majestic unseen. My voice and my approach broke the balance that had held her delicately on the border between this hot world and that. She leapt into the air as though released from a spring and she was dashed up against the side of the house, all four feet sprawling and scratching with claws spread out.

She fell from this height onto the ground and paused an instant, flat, her ears back, her head wagging from side to side, eyes searching an escape. From what? How should one know, this side of life?

Then she was off! She tore out into the empty space between us and the sage, and it became the wide race course where she circled round and round, trying to beat whatever raced with her. Faster and faster she covered the dusty ground, all proportion gone, all pleasant laws out of gear, harmony wiped away temporarily by a mischance of consciousness that had let down barriers for one small gray cat. As she passed us for the second time, the cook cried: "Fits!"

This effort to confine the mystery before us into a little medical term, annoyed me.

"And who knows what fits are?" I asked, thinking of Dostoievsky and the lightning that cracked through his brain.

The cook gave a small, almost imperceptible sniff.

"It's too hot," suggested Albidia.

The poor animal whirled at the third rounding of the course, ending where she had started, near us. She whirled on her tracks and rose right up into the air and seemed to split apart with some inner combustion, and from the height of a yard or so above the earth, she was released of the force that had been galvanizing her, and she fell like a plummet, hitting the ground with a soft thump. There she lay faintly jerking and twisting, her eyes rolled up so one saw just the whites of them.

"Oh! Call Max!" I exclaimed. "He will know what to do!" And Albidia went off in the sunshine to look for him down in the orchard.

But when he came and saw Kitty, just a gray bundle of rags, mechanically kicking with odd, weak movements, all resemblance to a pretty, glossy, smug cat wiped out, a broken diminished object, left there in the dust, he laughed a little ruefully and pushed his hat back on his wet hair and drew his hand across his forehead. Even as he did so the motion in her ceased quite suddenly and she was dead. The girls turned back into the house and Max went for the wheelbarrow.

"Too bad," Albidia said, consolingly, when she saw my face as I went through the swinging door into the dark dining room.

Presently she came in to where I was once more lying on the couch, in the room that seemed so cool and dim after the few moments outdoors.

"Here is a nice glass of lemonade," she said; "we thought maybe you'd like it."

I drank it gratefully. I was thinking of what extremes that poor Kitty had suffered in this world, of how I had found her nearly frozen one winter evening, and how the cold had given her that look of horror in her eyes, that was, perhaps, a premonition of the agony to be brought on by this summer's sun. Now she was gone and I had grown so fond of her and she of me. I had forgiven her so often for hunting the wild birds, and those others out there, those "pigeons on the grass! Alas!" that had always been her easy prey. Well, they would survive the longer after this, I thought, and I decided then I would never have another cat on this place. Let Kitty be the last.

But such decisions are of no avail, unfortunately. When the orange-colored kitten walked into Scott's garden over at Tony's house, could he send it flying? No, indeed. It became the household treasure. The good luck symbol, the pretty, petted kitty of the family there, no matter how many vases of flowers she tipped over and broke, no matter how she drove all the birds away out of the trees behind the house along the *acequia madre*. So do these little animals slide into our lives and join up with us. So do they assume significance and charm in our eyes!

"The yellow cat has had kittens!" bawls Scott over the telephone, in his beautiful voice, to Ralph far away in Los Angeles.

So life goes on!

Then the great Danes! Thyla and Donska are among the noblest, most loyal animals that I have ever had. They have an allegiance and a devotion to one that is rarely met with among human friends. Yet let them loose upon the place and they go tearing into the fields, tracking down the turkeys and the chickens until the hill is all in disturbance from the piercing squawks and shrieks from the flapping fowls, and the long, low baying of the dogs, ecstatic in pursuit. They love to run through the flower beds, leaving huge flat prints of their feet and crushing down the plants. As for the pigeons! The tame, unsuspicious pigeons! Every time she is out, Thyla creeps around the wall and seizes one in her wide jaws, crushes it and drops it and then slinks away, tail sagging, ears laid back, and a crafty, cold look in her yellow sidewise glance.

I have them penned up in the old Penitente Lodge that is now a garage and has a small room at its rear end with a wire enclosure opening out behind it, stretching to the high back *adobe* wall that runs along the back of the buildings. But they stand there all day looking out so wistfully, waiting for a glimpse of me, and wagging their long tails whenever anyone goes by, and that finally gets in on one. It is so sad for them to have to live like that. Then when they both come in heat in the summer season, what midnight howling around their home! What howling and prowling of all the dogs in the neighborhood! Thyla's son, "Big Boy," Donska's own brother, comes for two miles to visit them at the first intimation of their condition. What curious magnetism there is shown in this irrevocable attraction. What instinct and realization, surpassing the laws of thought and logic! We fancied the wire netting and the high wall were sufficient to segregate them, but alas! one morning Max found "Big Boy" inside the forbidden area, happy and carefree. So the weeks passed and it became evident that both the Danish girls were expecting! I was really confounded! I simply couldn't face any more Danes! They are so large, they eat so much, and what fun do they have? But I put off coping with the problem and let time roll on! Every time I saw them they smiled at me with confident faces and wagged their tails. I couldn't bear to think of what was coming.

But others did, and one day Cady told me of a friend who said she would gladly take them. They could range all about on her ranch and have a fine time. My heart contracted, but I said,

"All right! Tell her she can have them."

One day Cady telephoned me she had come for them. She had arrived in a beautiful big Packard sedan and she would take them away with her.

"All right," I answered. "Tell her to take them," and I went and shrank down in the couch and just waited for it to be over. I couldn't go out there and see them go and I hoped she'd hurry away!

In a moment I saw Thyla, with her head low, looking in the screen door. She saw me and grinned and wagged her tail, and I went to the door and she tried to come in, but I said:

"No, Thyla, go home (home!), go on back home," I repeated, patting her big smooth head for the last time. She gave me a queer long look and dropped her tail and turned around and walked very slowly out to the gate and out of sight. It gave me the meanest feeling, but I knew it was best for her.

They bundled the two of them into the back seat of the sedan and drove away. Afterwards we heard what hap-

EVENING OVER TAOS (*photograph by Edward Weston*)

TONY

pened. They stopped at the Columbian Hotel to get some supper before going on the hundred mile drive back to the ranch, and when they came back Thyla was having puppies on the velvet back seat, while Donska sat on her haunches, watching it all. She continued to have them until there were nine. Whether it was the shock of being taken away or because her time had come, we never knew. They all died, so I fear they were premature.

Two weeks later, I heard Donska had hers and they lived. The new owner told me over the telephone they are both happy and well and run all over the place. But I don't dare go and see them for fear of meeting Thyla's eyes. She may have been happy enough belonging to me, and living in a kennel. Dogs are strange that way.

But the lovely things of summer came back to me, too, as I dreamed on. How sometimes we cheat the sun by rising early in the lovely freshness of the morning and, hustling on a bathing suit and slippers, with clean clothes in a bright Mexican bag, drive over to the swimming pool at the Hot Spring. Over across to Ranchos and up to Llano and up the canyon till we come to the pocket in the hill where the fabulous water gushes forever out of the earth, hot, buoyant, sparkling, and radium charged, so they say.

A plunge into the hot pool inside the little building and then out to the air-cooled one that lies facing up to the sun! It is crystal clear, and a deep, limpid green. It shimmers and moves, perpetually shaken by the continuous gushing stream of the everlasting outpour. From where does it come, the rich pure water? What deep river far within the mountain furnishes so unending a life? For how long has this hurrying, tumbling element come spouting out of the darkness? And its source? What is its source? Can it go on like this forever? The purest, most pristine thing I have ever known is that pool, new in the morning, untouched, warm and alive.

It closes over one, and there is a kindness in the mild, soft feel of it, and no hardness of lime, but the benevolence of sodas and phosphates, soothing and strong.

It is lovely to float upon it, face turned up to the sun. It supports one easily and its buoyancy is such that one could not sink even if one wanted to. In fact, it is difficult to keep one's feet below the surface. But it is powerful and must be watched, for too long a time in it and one grows a little faint and weary. So swim back and forth and rest a few times and then come out and dress.

The drive back to the house, facing the Sacred Mountain all the way, is beautiful and dreamlike, for there is a faint rose and mauve haze over the hills and deep morning shadows in their canyons. The village of Taos, five miles away, is pearly, shining like cream along the low ridge upon which it is built, and the blue smoke from many fires curls up over the houses in the sunshine, and a few miles beyond it, lying low at the dark base of the mountain wall, the Pueblo is to be seen like two dim foothills of brown earth, bathed, too, in morning mists and cedar smoky veils.

How marvelous one's coffee tastes upon these occasions, with trays out on the platform with the brown stream running beneath it, and all the birds so gay in the branches overhead. The sun in the east shines through the hollyhocks and they are a bright, bright curtain between us and the house, made of little lamps strung up and down upon the stout stalks. Brightest red and yellow and pink, and lavender, at the edge of the dark island where we sit, burning to hurt the eyes, while under the trees we are all in green shadow, eating our eggs and bacon, buttered toast and marmalade, with our heads still wet and our faces cool.

Another way to forget the warm weather is to go right out into it in the daytime. This is just the opposite from the dim withdrawal into the darkened rooms of the house where hardly a sound is to be heard, save a lazy fly whirling around overhead, or the distant mowing machine out in the fields, or one of the girls singing far away in the

kitchen. There is an utter peace and pleasure in lying re-
laxed upon the cool taffeta of the couch in the living room,
with barely enough light to read by, but enough, light
enough to read Blake's poems from the big volume

("... Love that never told shall be as the gentle
wind that moves
Silently, invisibly. . . .")

With one's handkerchief damp with lavender water, and
a tall pitcher of iced tea, with lemon and mint sprigs in it,
standing on the little table beside one. On the little table,
in addition to the iced tea there are cigarettes and matches,
all kinds of cigarettes, the plain white package of Chester-
fields, the buff one with the Camel on it (though really
sometimes one feels one would walk a mile to get away
from that Camel), and the Benson and Hedges Ambar
cigarettes that Cady sent for. There are the little pearl and
silver Georgian fruit knife and fork that Carl found in the
Caledonian market for me, the Indian silver cigarette holder
Adrian gave me on his last day here, the little watch, with
the thick, black enamel covers that slide over the face of
it that Stanislav gave Tony and that I took for myself, and
all the little tortoise shell, silver, enamel and wooden boxes
people have sent, and they lie there in a patient row, and
they contain pins, bits of turquoise, little sticks of osha
root, beads that fall from broken chains, and small parts
of old, useless jewelry. Then there is a bottle of lavender

salts and a bottle of Guerlain's "Pois de Senteur." (How lovely it is, too!) How can one small table hold so many things? There is, besides, a green vase of double nasturtiums and violas, and a disheveled box of Baur's French-mints, the most suave candy in the world that not only melts in your mouth, but while you look at it! All these things gathered slowly together, parts of the whole that is one's environment, little things that take the hard edges off life, they make the charm of a warm summer afternoon in the house.

But I don't know whether the other kind is not more memorable. The picnic! With so many high glades and mountain brooks to choose from that one hardly knows which to go to. Shall we drive up to Frieda's, and sit under the pine trees near the Gallina Creek and listen to the wind in the branches while we look down, down, down over the pale valley that pulsates below one, and almost, almost see Lorenzo coming to meet us, his blue shirt in and out between the red spruce tree trunks? The crows fly among the tree tops, cawing, cawing, and the grasses of the mountainside are sprinkled with wild Lupin flowers and that spiky stalk with small red bells up and down it that Lawrence always called "the little scarlet rain." Or shall we ride our horses up to Glorietta and lie on the smooth grassy earth and look far up into the ancient trees of that sacred grove where Indians have had their picnics for centuries before us? It is very pastoral and poetic here, making one think of Scythia.

Out from the dark forest, little boys soon join us, staring at our feast with round, black-eyed interest. The sandwiches and stuffed eggs, cookies and fruit will have to be shared, so we take more than we need for ourselves. We linger on the mead longer and longer, loath to move, and we watch the shadows grow black and straight as the sun moves over the high canopy of the cottonwoods. The horses over beyond crop the short grass all the afternoon, occasionally stamping to dislodge a fly, flapping their tails as they munch, munch, munch indefatigably, with a watchful eye upon us. When it is cool, we ride them home; we ride right into the sunset and the sun is level with us on the far horizon, and the sagebrush smells sweet under the horses' hooves.

Fast, fast, we canter home in the evening and it is a race with the sun, sinking so fast over there; the western sky has a tumbled mass of clouds across it, all orange and violet and deep red edged with copper and the Sacred Mountain, behind, is a flushed fiery rose for a moment. What privilege in the world is like this one, to move with this gayety through the sumptuous afterglow when the valley is all a warm bloom of light?

Suddenly we look in amazement at the eastern hills, upon our right. They are now the coldest olive green against a dark, cold blue sky. Over them snow-white clouds, solid as frozen worlds, boil and hover. The invulnerable east that escapes the evening fires! "Oh, world, as God has made it . . . !"

Other days it's fishing! "They" are going fishing and we will go along. Then we have to motor up the Hondo Canyon to Twining, nine miles above this valley, high up in the aspens, where the trail starts over to Wheeler's Peak along the high, treeless ridge, over to Blue Lake and its unearthly mystery. The rough, stony road winds and curves up through the strong forest where vast landslides of rock and gravel show here and there on the steep sides; the pine trees mixed with spruce and evergreen are hoary and rugged, and every kind of wild flower blooms in turn at their feet along the water. It is a wild, tough mountain, this one, and it smells of ancient damp leaf mold and faint new blossoms. It is the forest primeval persisting still in the face of men, the life in it vigorous and aloof. It is the same now as it was before men built a gold- and copper-mining town at the head of the canyon and called it Twining and raised log cabins and saloons and a long, low hotel, and failed to overcome the natural resistance of the place and its remoteness. Now there is no sign left of that undertaking except some vast, forlorn, moss-covered machinery, and a charred woodpile of many tons of cordwood that was set on fire and destroyed, but the mountain is still safe and solid.

The Hondo River is a fierce, small stream, tumbling over big rocks and there are nine bridges across it before we reach the end. In this icy water the trout lie dreaming and frisking, and up and down, up and down the damp mossy banks tramp the fishermen casting their lines.

I never fish, but I love to walk around and pick the wild, mauve columbines and look for wild strawberries, and find on the white tree trunks the initials of John carved in the soft bark so many years ago, his own and Betty's woven inside a heart! And then to lie on the ground, face down, close to it, so one can actually feel the powerful vibrations of the earth pass into one, like waves of strong music. High above one in the blue sky between the dark, wooded canyon walls sometimes an eagle or a hawk swims and soars, or a faint wild singing comes down to one, piercing and sweet, and the whole of summer seems condensed into that happy sound. And under that singing there is the perpetual humming and crooning of the forest, the sound of the trees and the insects, and a constant flutter and jump, a skipping and a flying from innumerable little things, squirrels, chipmunks, flickers, and other wild birds; the darting dragon flies on the quieter pools, the spiders, ants, bees and beetles that dart here and there, living their lives more purposefully, perhaps, than ourselves, who encroach upon them.

Then the odd creatures! The brown twigs that walk, the green leaves that fly away, and the spider, like a piece of bark that gazes at one cross-eyed and motionless and then startles one by suddenly crawling up the tree!

We have brought books, but we never read them, there is so much to watch and hear, and presently the long afternoon fades away, and when it is dusk, with the sun a gold rim on the upper edges of the slopes, and the sky all full of rosy clouds floating across the highest peaks above us, the fishermen return and throw themselves down beside us and give a detailed account of the behavior of every fish they saw, and we must be patient with them. And we are.

On such a picnic we have our supper there where we spent the day, cooking it on a big fire of dried pine wood. Coffee strong and good, beefsteaks hung on crotched sticks with the fat dripping and sizzling, and a fine loaf of brown, home-made bread that we tear into chunks. Some like big round slices of raw onions dipped in salt to eat with it— I do!

The night comes down fast in the canyon, and soon it is quite dark and stars shine in the somber sky. The air is icy then and our backs grow cold, so we huddle in blankets while we are too toasted in front. There is not much talking; generally someone is cross, but that's all right, too.

"Well—there are five small trout for you in the creel, Mabel," Andrew says.

"Goody! Goody! Goody!" One every morning for breakfast for five days. He knows I love better than almost anything in this life, a small crisp trout fried in cornmeal, black coffee, and raisin bread toast for breakfast, and almost all summer he keeps me supplied, and that's the right kind of a friend of twenty-five years' standing!

So many kinds of picnics, I cannot tell of them all! Up Taos Canyon and over to the Eagle Nest Lake in Moreno Valley, where one goes in a boat after salmon trout, up the Rio Chiquito, over the U. S. Hill to Mora, where one spreads luncheon out in the old churchyard, a bottle of white wine, honey and rolls, cheese and olives and cold chicken under the eyes of all the kids in the village. The churchyard is wide and shady and has a wall around it and it is strangely serene for such a curious narrow valley framed in harsh, beautiful, jagged mountain peaks.

And we can never forget Red River over beyond the north range, that old mining town, with its rotting wooden stores, abandoned in the sun, their false fronts rising so straight and weathered to a dark gray. When we go to spend a summer day on the long circle drive around the mountains, we have to lunch at the "Home of the Hot

Biscuits" where darling old Mrs. Brandenburg brings us three platters of small fried chickens and we eat dozens of the famous biscuits with home-made grape jelly on them. Then home through the aspens, the little maidens with their slim white poles, green leaves all twittering.

Oh, there is so much nature in this neighborhood I live in! Sometimes I want to forget it for an hour, then I call up Helen or Myrtle and we go down to the Tavern in the Plaza and sit at a dark table in the long, cool room and order beer on draught and pretzels, and look out of the window and see all the cars raising dust and that is good, too, in its own way once in a while.

Usually we have two rainy seasons; a short one in June, when the first crop of alfalfa is ready to cut, and the other in August when the second cutting is ready. As water ruins alfalfa and two times out of three we have to bring ours in damp and stack it so, or turn it in the fields so many times, all the life has been crushed out of it, or baling it, have the bales turn to dust inside and give the horses the heaves, I have tried to decide not to have any more but instead to plow it up and to persuade Tony to plow his up and plant meadow hay instead.

Alfalfa is better for cows than horses anyway. But we

have so much the habit of alfalfa that it is difficult to change, and when I try to argue about it with Tony, he says:

"I taught you all you know about farmin' and now you better farmer than me?"

So things go on as they always have gone. But aside from that, the rainy season is delicious. The mornings are resplendent, so bright and clear, with every particle of dust washed away, and then at quite a regular hour in the afternoon between three and six, the huge round white clouds that have been rolling along all day spread over the sky and the rain falls effortlessly and makes everything sparkle and shine when the sun comes out again before sunset. Sometimes there is a cloudburst and the water suddenly falls upon us in a solid mass as though some vast reservoir had opened. In a few moments, thick streams are pouring out of the *canalies* on the roofs, rivers run down from the desert behind the house, lakes form in the low spots, and when it is over, as quickly as it came, the flowers are all lying down and the world seems like one vast mud puddle. It soaks quickly into the earth and by morning there is nothing to show for it.

It is lovely to go out on the horses in the rain, with the big yellow slickers covering us completely, and to trot briskly through the soft, slushy fields, or to gallop over to the *mesa* along the country road across two or three streams, splash, the water striking us on our faces, and throwing mud on our boots.

We ride with the rain beating down on our eyes, along the top of the *mesa* that runs across the valley west of the village. The clouds are low all around us, obscuring the mountains and the hills, and the world is changed into a vast, gray, misty plain without form or feature, soundless save for our passage through it. The warm summer rain trickles down over our faces, down inside our collars and the horses steam. The wet, trampled sage smells wonderful. When we speak, our voices sound muffled and faraway to each other and we are laughing with pleasure in wetness, the soaking wetness, and the refreshment of it in our high, dry climate. Our hair is plastered down on our heads, my red ribbon is soggy, my hands grow chilly and the bridle reins are sticky. We race our horses with our eyes shut and they slide precariously in the slippery clay. Never mind! We are exhilarated and made happy by the rain and we lose our heads a little.

It grows dark early on these wet afternoons, and we ride home in a somber, purple twilight. Then a hot bath, a clean gingham dress, and a highball, and by that time the sun has slashed through the ominous, dark-gray, western sky, cutting it like a sword that divides a heavy mantle. The rooms are suddenly filled with light and when I go to the door and look out there is the world all jeweled, every leaf, every twig, and flower and stone glinting and throwing out prismatic flashes, and behind the house an enormous double rainbow arches across the sky from the Pueblo to the peak of Mirador.

Mirador is the highest hill behind our house. Sometimes we ride up to the top of it through brush and close grown trees, and a steep trail that is nearly obliterated now.

In the old days when the Indians returned from hunting expeditions they came up from the east out of Taos Canyon to cross the mountains and from the summit of this high point they could see the Pueblo far away down below at the foot of the Sacred Mountain.

They would light a signal fire to tell their families they had come back and the people of the village would come along the trail to meet them, singing. So, when the Spaniards first came here they named the mountain Mirador, which means Lookout. The signal fires never burn up there any more, but one finds traces of the old flames burned black in the rocks at the top of the bare open spaces, where on one side the whole Taos Valley is lying unfurled like a lovely embroidery down below, and on the other one can look thousands of feet down into the Canyon and distinguish automobiles like tiny insects scrambling along the winding road that leads over to Moreno Valley and thence to Raton.

In some years when we suffer from drought, it is quite

another story and then we miss our rain terribly. The summer droops and grows pallid with dust, the Rio Grande down below dwindles and narrows and runs listlessly to the Gulf, and up here in our valley all the little streams show the rocks they usually cover with the bubbling water. Dust hangs like a pall over everything and stifles the garden and the crops. Our *acequia* runs sullenly at first ("Wind, do some*thing* to these waters!") and gradually diminishes. Then the *Major Domo* and the Indians begin to ration it out, so that it only runs through our place certain days a week, and finally only one day a week, or one night. Farmers begin to grow testy and irritable over water. They meet at the head-gates with their shovels and hoes and break into angry disputes. Anger increases as the water diminishes and fights begin. People kill for water in this country, and the tension increases with the drought so that one doesn't see many smiling faces any more down our way, except on the Indians. I have never seen a look of anxiety or exasperation over any kind of weather on an Indian face. Whatever comes in Nature they meet it with acceptance as though it were right. They do not know how to resist natural things like drought or hail or cloudbursts with anger and hate because they are so much at one with all the elements. They know they are themselves the earth and the rain and the sun and when the sun sets they feel the peace and rightness of it. They watch the sun going down behind the horizon and they go down with it in a participation with its security and its gentle irrevocable progress that we have no experience of. We watch things happen in Nature as though they were outside us and separate from us, but the Indians know they are that which they contemplate.

One may meet an Indian after a violent summer storm and after our manner, one is apt to refer to it with a look of doom and a shaking head and words like: "That was a terrible fall of hail we had the other day!" Then, as like as not, the Indian will look up into the sky with a loving smile and reply:

"Yes. I lost all my corn," and laugh a little out loud and maybe shake his head a little, too, with a sort of condonation of the mischievousness of it, but with no rancor and no worry. Natural weather just can't worry them, they have so much faith in Nature and in themselves. Will we ever recover our lost adjustment to this elemental life, or arrive at a new one so that we know everything is for the best in the best of worlds?

When we have a season of drought, it changes everything. Sounds, smells, colors, all are different. We hear everything much plainer, so that our voices are heard from house to house across the field, and every animal noise seems accentuated.

The air acquires a heavy odor of dust, an indescribable smell that is mixed with ripening fruit, and flowers, with occasional whiffs, all the way from the corral, of pigs and goats and horses. When one snatches leaves off the sagebushes riding through them, and crushes them for their scent, the first sniff is the dusty smell, the smell one has to swallow in everything. And as in this place, flowers, fruit, vegetables, onions, apples, peaches, pumpkins, all growing things, have a far stronger flavor than those grown in the lowlands, so the very earthen dust of which these things are composed has a sort of fierce tang and flavor to it, not altogether unpleasant, in fact, characteristic and familiar and homogeneous.

There is a veil of warm, pink-yellow dust covering everything, mellowing the bright, hard summer colors, and softening every outline. In the distance the hills have a blue haze over them that turns to violet in the evening, and the Sacred Mountain looks like a vast purple blossom, with all its petals open to the sky.

Against the sinking sun, between us and the west, veil on veil of soft, pastel-colored dust hide the brilliance of the sky; they hang like sheaths across the orange ball, dimming its rays so it seems to be a concrete, round, red-hot planet falling with a singular imperturbability, through the long banks of lavender and rose to the faint, low blue hills on the skyline. Wonderful days for painters, these days of drought! But behind the beauty there are other realities: hunger and want.

The animals suffer first. Up in the hills there is not enough water, the berries do not mature, the grass dries up. This drives them down to the valley. The bears and their cubs travel down the slopes and try to reach water at night and return at dawn to their hiding places. We find great tracks, like the hands of a giant man along the ditch, and sometimes we wake at night and the wild, musty smell that means bear comes up to the open window. We know there are bears around the house at night and Scott heard one growl and grumble outside his door. They turn over the garbage pails, they trample down the sunflowers in the little *arroyo* behind the Two Story House, and everyone walks warily when they go home at night, taking care to throw the beam of their flashlight into all the shadows. It would not be very amusing to walk into the arms of a bear unexpectedly in the dark, although it does sound funny. When Andrew went outdoors one sweet morning he found the little wooden toilet cocked over, one side up off the ground. The bear had taken it in his stride and had not bothered to move out of the way.

Scott had Eliseo come down and stay up all night waiting for a sight of the animal. He sat outside in the automobile with his gun loaded, but there wasn't a sign of bear.

" 'Course not," scoffed Tony. "Think bears like the smell of guns?"

All over the valley other people shot bears in their villages, though nobody told who, for there is one of those odd laws in existence here that if you want to shoot a certain bear you have to write to Santa Fe and get a permit to do it, and people generally don't wait for that. They are afraid for their children. They all know that bears especially love babies and small children and will steal them if they can. A Navajo friend of mine told me he knows of nine or ten cases where bears have stolen Navajo babies and suckled them and taken care of them, and whenever a child disappears the Navajos hunt the bear. In only one or two cases the child was found dead.

One early morning after a rain, I was riding across the Pueblo Road to go over to Spud's, and I saw a couple of Indians laughing together and looking down at it, and when I went over they showed me the great, fresh, deep-clawed imprints of the bear where she had crossed Highway 64, which is what tourists call that old road, and the little marks of the cub coming behind.

One of the nicest things we do in the summer in the short period when it has grown warm and dry on the ground, and before the cold weather comes at the end of August, is to go up to Blue Lake for a night and a day and we leave early in the morning when there is a dew sparkling on everything and cobwebs stretching all in one direction across the grasses and trees. We take the long trail behind the Pueblo Mountain for twenty-five miles; we plod, with our camping things on pack horses behind us, and it is a slow ride, for we can rarely go beyond a walk, and only occasionally into the jog trot.

We leave behind us everything that we love in houses and gardens and all we have is what the Indians say God gave them: "Just what grows on the mountain." But the richness of it! The mountainsides are covered with patches of mauve-blue columbine and the "little scarlet rain" and all the other flowers. The forests are deep in vivid green moss and dozens of varieties of birds sing on all sides. The vividness of all this growing life is startling when one leaves furniture and curtains, silk and cloth and made things behind one.

The little river is beside us until we climb above it, and we hear it below in the crevices of the giant hills. After a while, as we go higher and higher, the color fades out of the sunshine so it is as though everything is drawn in black and white! The trail leads up into the very high mountains that tumble and billow, roll on roll beyond us. We never see anyone except an occasional Indian wrapped in his white sheet riding over the slopes.

Sometimes across a deep abyss an Indian, so far away over on the opposite mountainside I cannot even see him, will accost us with a call like a bird, and Tony and Trinidad will answer him with their hands cupping their mouths.

Sound grows strange up on these heights. It seems squeezed and solid. Our voices are unfamiliar to us and we do not talk much.

By noon we reach the halfway place where the tribe stops on the first halt when it makes the journey up to Blue Lake for its great August Ceremony.

Here there is a spring so we can drink and water our horses, and we like to lie on the ground a while to rest our tired backs, and then we eat our dinner.

Tony is a fine camp cook and makes good grilled steaks, fried potatoes and onions and coffee, and soon we are rested and ready to go on.

Our little string of horses are like ants crawling over these enormous spaces. The trail winds around mountain after mountain and in some places it is cut into the steep sides until there is just a narrow shelf to ride on with the earth rising perpendicular and straight up above one on one hand and on the other falling away so abruptly one looks down past the horse into miles of green bottomless darkness. This part of the ride is always a little frightening, and one leans as far as possible towards the mountain; one can reach out and touch it with one's hand! Looking back, one sees the bulging packs on the pack horses are hanging right out over the abyss.

We took Brett up there once and she prepared herself for her customary vertigo in high places by carrying a long rope and a policeman's whistle. When we reached the first steep mountain where we had to crawl around the ledge, she roped herself to Trinidad who rode ahead of her. She tied her rope around her waist and gave him the other end which he carried in his hand. Then, she shut her eyes and sat.

However, she made the mistake of opening them too soon and caught a sudden glimpse down into those depths! We heard the shrill whistle blasting the terrible summits and Trinidad singing against it. Looking back, we saw him laughing and Brett blowing for all she was worth to hearten herself and show us how she felt.

Upon one of these mountainsides the osha plant grows. It has stalks and leaves like celery and the root is wonderful to burn in the house, for it has a sweet, heavy, oriental perfume, like an incense, and it obliterates all other stale smells of cigarettes or cooking. The Indians use it for colds and sore throats, chewing it and swallowing the juice, which is very spicy and sharp and stings one's mouth. It is considered a very powerful medicine, for snakes, witches and other harmful entities cannot endure it. When Autumn comes we get an Indian boy to go up and dig a sackful of roots for us that we burn on winter evenings and we never have known anyone who did not love its lovely fragrance.

The afternoon passes, the light fades, and evening is coming when we are upon the cold, treeless ridges in austerity and awe, utterly removed from everyday life and everything we are used to in light and sound. As we top the last bleak, shale-covered edge we see below us Blue Lake. Bottomless, peacock blue, smooth as glass, it lies there like an uncut, shining jewel. Symmetrical pine trees, in thick succession, slope down to its shores in a rapid descent on three sides.

This Blue Lake is the most mysterious thing I have ever seen in nature, having an unknowable, impenetrable life of its own, and a definite emanation that rises from it. Here is the source of most of the valley life. From this unending water supply that flows out of the east end of the lake and down the miles and miles of the rocky bed of the stream to the Pueblo, the Indian fields are irrigated. It is turned into the *acequia madre*, that winds on down through the Indian land until it reaches the town and feeds all our fields and orchards that lie on the eastern side of the valley. The west portion of the valley is watered from Bear Lake, another deep pool with a perpetual spring feeding it.

The Indians call this one Star Water, it is so light and clear. Near the opening of the canyon there is a little, sheltered glade where the Indian sweet grass grows and of it they make bundles to perfume their clothes.

It has never been surprising to me that the Indians call

Blue Lake a sacred lake, and worship it. Indeed, at first I felt we should not camp upon its shore, but after I found out how they conduct the camp there I knew it was all right and fitting that one should sleep beside it and try to draw what one could for oneself from its strong being.

The evening fire is soon burning and the food ready; the Indians are speaking in low voices that yet are very distinct at that altitude of nearly fourteen thousand feet, and the horses are hobbled and we hear them crunching their oats over in the trees. When the dishes are washed and all the scraps are burned and we are sitting in a circle around the fire, the Indians begin to chant, at first in faint, humming tones, that gradually grow strong and full. They look over to the lake and sing to it. Their faces show they are deep in communion with the place they are in. They experience it and adore it as we do not know how to do.

The dark night is soon full of the repeated mantric song. The sound of it goes back and forth between the singers and the mountains, the lake and the fire. They go on singing for hours, long after I have gone into the pine shelter and wrapped myself in blankets to go to sleep. It isn't easy to sleep as high as that, but to lie awake in the marvelous air and feel the potency of the place has a kind of active repose in it and one is always refreshed by the night up there.

Riding back to the valley late the next day has the same

surprise in it every time. The fields of corn and wheat that we ride through seem terribly rich and luxurious and there is a thickness of living in the downy, sumptuous, golden valley. When we reach our house in the dusk, the living room seems crowded with comforts, the bright colors and glints of metal and glass startle one whose eyes, just in those few hours, grew used to the holy look of natural life. Most of us are used only to the awesome holiness of churches and lofty arches, cathedrals where, with stained glass and brooding silences, priests try to emulate the religious atmosphere that is to be found in the living earth in some of her secret places. . . .

Something bumped against the window with a sudden whack. A bird flying towards the light? It startled me back to the present and I turned over the books beside me. I tried to read first one and then another. One of the detective stories was a good one, the kind that is well enough written so one can go off into the environment of it and, entering a different world, be lost for a while to the present. So I read on and on, and in between times heard the maids passing in a procession through the dining room, having locked the kitchen doors, on their way home to the cottage they sleep in across the alfalfa field.

So now the house sank into a deeper silence, and presently I stopped reading and my mind got away from me and I began imagining things.

I knew how slippery the roads must be out there on the way back from Seco, and I had a vision of Tony's car overturned in a ditch with him pinned inside it and no one passing. Perhaps badly hurt, perhaps freezing to death if no one came to help before the next day.

I reminded myself I had had these fears for years and years whenever Tony was out late, and they had never been true. He is a good, careful driver and takes no chances. But yet, the time might come when it *would* be true. He should have been back long before now—when it is nearly ten o'clock at night.

Whatever has he been doing all day? I pondered all the possibilities that might attend the trading of a sack of oats! One thing leads to another. Perhaps someone gave him a drink of bad whiskey; perhaps he was blind by this time!

Then the Indians. . . . In these months they have their quarrels and arguments. If there are any troubles, they come in February. In March they begin to plow and everything like that fades away. But now it was February. What if some enemy of Tony's met him at night on the road and— But no, I persuaded myself, they are not like that. But aren't they? How does one know?

I got up and walked downstairs through the empty house.

Flowers bloomed, stilly, in the Big Room, the fire burned softly in the fireplace, and the feeling of it was nice. But so empty!

I remembered summer days and how different the house was then: our dining room is always cool and dim and rather like a pleasant tomb in the summer. The wild olive tree outside one of the west windows hangs its thick pale leaves against the panes and the other windows in the eastern alcove, as well as the long French window, are veiled with full gauze curtains, the color of burnt sienna, to tune in with the red-brown and black tiles on the floor. These tiles were made behind the house one year and they are polished glossy with beeswax every few days. The ceiling is like the one in the Laguna church, the saplings painted with earth colors, sienna red and white earth, and lampblack, in stripes of four saplings to each color, so that it looks like an Indian blanket. The walls are whitewashed, of course, and they are gray and shadowy in the subdued light. Mary built the fireplace years ago, or at least she built one there in the alcove between the two long, narrow windows, but Tony came in and looked at it and went out and got a little ax and chopped it down and built it up again to suit himself.

In the winter, our round dining-room table is shoved over near the fireplace, between the two, white-painted, wooden posts that support the beams of the alcove, but in the summertime it is pushed into the center of the room. But sometimes summer comes so quickly and things begin to go so fast that we forget to move it and it just stays there in the south end where it was in the quiet wintertime.

For, in the summer, the house is always full of people and we rarely sit down to dinner with fewer than six or eight at the table, and the same happens often unexpectedly for lunch, people arriving from all over the world. Because I do not like to have many different people at one time, losing the flavor of all of them in the mêlée, purposely I have a table that only holds eight and in this way no one is lost. But even so, only one meal a day in company! No matter how many or who is in the dining room in the summertime, my lunch is brought to me on a tray in the living room and I eat it there on a little old table. I do not know why I do this but I suppose it is because I had so many meals on a tray in my nursery when I was a child and they were invariably pleasanter and more peaceful that the ones I took with the grown-ups who, apparently, only met in the dining room and took that opportunity to air their grievances.

As it was, I imagine that then I learned that habit of impatience to be gone from the table, that rides me yet, and has me on the edge of my chair, ready to rise, while everyone else is lingering as long as possible over the sweets!

There is no reason on earth to hurry, for from the moment of the cocktails in there among the flowers, with the sweet evening air, freshened after sunset, blowing through the long room, it is surely one of the nicest times in the day for me, always the hungry time, for a salad and tea at noon makes one extremely interested in food by seven o'clock!

Bourbon and grapefruit juice and mint leaves freshly picked along the ditch, shaken up with ice cubes until the glass shaker is frosty, and along with this, summer muslins and perfume—laughter and fun, with the antagonisms forgotten for a moment and everyone gathered together in a good humor, this Big Room that was so hushed and shaded two or three hours ago would not be known for the same place, all sparkling now under the lights, with the spots of bright color starting out, some among the paler grays and yellows of the chairs and couches which hold here a brightly somber magenta satin cushion gleaming, there one of emerald green, and others on the tables where there are bowls of sweet peas and roses, and tall vases filled with vivid gladioli that Eliseo grew in his country house garden and brings to me every week or so.

On the long, dark, scarred table under the west window at the left of the front door, always open day and night upon the long portal, there are a couple of rows of books, one in front of the other, the new books that will presently be shifted out to the book room. Such a mixture, too! The last mystery story, the last scientific premise, the last mystical doctrine, the last hard-boiled novel, and all the new books friends have sent this year with tender inscriptions in them. These last will not stay here very long! It is remarkable how autographed books fade away and turn up in collections! On a long shelf that sets up on the back of the table there is a row of Lorenzo's books, all autographed, that he sent me at different times from different parts of the world, and these I try to hold on to. And some of the translations of them into other languages that Frieda has given me are here too, looking so odd in Polish or Scandinavian! Brett's book about him is here and Frieda's and mine, too, and the others, Carswell's, Murry's, Seligman's, Ada's, Miriam's, and the Brewsters'. What a row! He would laugh and make a face if he saw them, and perhaps he does!

Even on summer nights there is apt to be a fire in the fireplace, and Pooch lying in front of it, calmly certain no one will step on her, and no one does, though skirts brush across her nose and she gives a little moan. There are some strange and inexplicable objects grouped around this chimney place and once in a while I catch a stranger's eyes fixed upon it with a puzzled look.

There is, for instance, a battered metal ear trumpet hanging from the electric light sconce, and a real heirloom this,

CHURCH AT RANCHOS DE TAOS
(*photograph by Carl Van Vechten*)

MABEL'S BELOVED BIRD HOUSE

the one Brett brought first to Taos, and a dozen little Chinese objects in wood that Mary brought me from Peiping, each one signed with the artist's initials; they are supposed to be fastened in the tail feathers of the pigeons to make music when they fly—then there are nine, small, carved, ivory skulls from the bottom of crucifixes in Italy. There is a wild duck made of baked clay, there is a stone heart found in front of the house, and beside it a small copper crucifixion from the Anaconda mine in Butte, Montana. Over all these, a tall, dark, delicate wooden carving of Buddha stands, looking out across to the front door, with his fingers raised in the gesture of submission, and on the other side of the chimney a fine photograph of Tony looks benign, and Egyptian, owing to the straight folds of his blanket, which cuts right down from the side of his head across his chest.

Andrew was gazing at all these unrelated objects the other day and laughing: "Your chimney place begins to look like Lourdes or some place like that. Where people hang their crutches and go away cured!"

"I hope cured!" I replied.

Exactly at seven the bell is rung in the dining room and out we go. If anyone is late that is just too bad, for we never wait. A good dinner, carefully prepared, should be eaten when it is ready.

On the "Lazy Sally" that Alice gave me years ago are

waiting dishes of such good things as mustard pickles, rather sweet, made of small onions, cucumbers and cauliflower, transparent green mint jelly, whole-wheat raisin bread, hot biscuits and fresh butter, all home-made, and stalks of crisp celery, stuffed with cream cheese, and a saucer of green chili.

The green chili has a long home history with us. We buy its parent string once a year down in the lower valley at Velarde. It is a heavy garland of vermilion red chili, weighing over a hundred pounds and we buy it for a dollar and hang it beside the front door for a San Gerónimo Fiesta decoration.

It grows darker and darker as it dries there, and looks more than ever like glossy patent leather. But when winter comes and it is all shriveled and rattling, Max carries it into the back storeroom and hangs it from a beam. All winter it is ground into powder for *chili con carne* which we crave every ten days or so, and when spring comes, and the ground is ready, Max plants what is left of the seed in the withered, blackened pods down in the orchard in neat rows. All summer they flourish and when the plants have the chili pods lengthening on them in August, we can eat them as a relish, skinned by parching them on top of the stove so that their strange, subtle perfume is forced out, and then stewed with a little olive oil and garlic.

As likely as not we will have lamb for dinner, brought

down from Tony's ranch at Tienditas, potatoes grown at the same place, baked squash with raisins in the hollow, lettuce and cucumbers and tomato salad with imported olive oil and lemon dressing, and for dessert a brown Betty pudding with hard sauce. All these things will come from our orchard. The winter apples are not good to eat yet, but they are all right for cooking. We will pick them in a little while. No one can call this kind of dinner either exciting or elaborate, but cooked as our Beatrice cooks for us in the summer when she is with us, it is perfectly excellent, and everybody invariably takes two helpings of every single thing.

When we have squabs from the dovecotes out in the garden, and small creamed onions, shoestring potatoes and crabapple jelly, and in addition, just for fun, broiled mushrooms, with a salad of celery and nuts and apples smeared with home-made mayonnaise dressing, one can feel one's cup is just about running over, especially with a cheese-cake for dessert. I have never seen happier faces bending over food than at our table, where the big round shade over the electric lights hangs above us and softens everything.

Pooch sits on the cold tiles beside one or the other of these people she knows so well, her ears cocked and three perpendicular wrinkles show between her bulging eyes. She gazes into faces and tries to will them to drop her a sliver once in a while. Her mouth waters unfortunately, and a long loop of saliva hangs from her lips.

These summer nights the windows are open, east and west. On the east side one can see the moon come bounding over the black hill from where we sit, and on the west side the scent of the flowers outside comes into the room to mix with the smell of sweet grass that has been packed in the ceiling above the saplings. In the corner of the room a big bundle of sweet clover hangs from a beam. We always pick it early in the summer and hang it in the rooms to discourage flies, for they are said to hate it.

After dinner, coffee and liqueurs back in the big happy living room, and in the evening what? Someone turns on the radio, or someone returns to the dining room to play the piano; when the company is that way, childish games are produced, though, thank God, not often. I hate all games so! However, if others come in during the evening, guessing games are a help to bind things together.—("You go out—no, you—")

If Tony is there he usually sets up the card table and plays solitaire in silence, and later refers to the more or less brilliant conversation that has taken place as "flies buzzing!" I have long since given up trying to explain Tony and my friends to each other. Sometimes they take to each other and sometimes they do not, and they rarely understand each other even when they do!

All through the year he goes about visiting other tribes, especially at Fiesta times when many of them are gathered together. He has been building up the solidarity between them for twenty years, for when he forfeited many of his Pueblo activities by coming with me, he turned outwards, and began working in a larger circle. Lately he told me he thought God had brought us together, so he would be turned to the outside work for Indians.

For a long time he interpreted Collier to them, in faraway places where the latter had not had a chance yet to make a contact.

Since Collier became Indian commissioner, Tony has been working among the Indians, interpreting his efforts to preserve the Indian life and culture. He is always on his job, thinking about it and planning even when he is playing solitaire in his solitary silence in the midst of my friends.

"Sometimes Tony irritates me," said one of them to me. "He seems to live such an *unmotivated* existence!"

When Tony came back from Hopiland where John Collier sent him to instruct the Indians in one of the safeguarding efforts being made for them, he dictated the following letter to me:

MY DEAR JOHN:

Last summer when I went to the Snake Dance, I talked with Fred Kabotie of Chimopavi about the Wheeler-Howard Bill. He told me then, it was impossible to have an organization, on account of they're living far apart in separate pueblos. At that time, Fred said that all the old people were against that Bill and did not believe in in.

This time when I went, on the 15th of November, I went first to Hotevilla and I asked how I could arrange to get a meeting to talk about the Wheeler-Howard Bill. They told me to go and see the Chief about it for that is all they have—just a Chief. I went to see the Chief to ask him to have the meeting and he asked me if I had any right to come there and do that kind of work. I hadn't the recommendation of the agent that day. I just said I had the Bill you sent me, signed John Collier, and I told him, "I am coming from John Collier and he signed this Bill," and I showed him the sign.

The Chief then told me he would call a meeting for the afternoon.

I went up at two o'clock and there was no sound of any meeting. I went again to the Chief and then he began to call the people.

The ones that were there that day came and I explained to them what the Bill meant, and all about Self-Government. I told them how the Rio Grande Indians rule by self-government, by having a Governor and a Lieutenant-governor and the twelve officers. And the War Chief has a Lieutenant and he has twelve members for himself. I explained what the War Chief has to do.

The War Chief has to take care of and look after all the land outside, look after the boundaries and their fences, and the Governor takes care of everything inside the village, family troubles and the way the people must behave. He

216

has the same power as a white man's judge or justice of the peace. He can fine the people if they don't obey the rules, and everybody knows the rules for they are old rules.

Besides the Governor, there is the Council. The Council is made up of those who have been governors, lieutenant-governors, war chiefs and his lieutenants. If anything goes wrong, the Governor calls the Council together in his house to talk it over. Or if there is any important business of letter to talk over or a visit from somebody to do with the village affairs, he calls the Council together. The Council decides everything by a majority vote. After the Council decides questions, the Governor signs.

I told them that is the power of Self-Government.

And I told them to look ahead and see that, maybe some-time, some Secretary of the Interior could allot Indian land to separate Indians and pretty soon they would have noth-ing, but if they decide to have Self-Government under the Wheeler-Howard Bill, they are safe, forever. To be safe, they have to be a community like we are and have rulers.

I told them how about twice a year we have All-Pueblo meetings at Santo Domingo where we talk over different business that effects us. Each Governor of a Pueblo sends two or three delegates of the best men to these All-Pueblo meetings. I told them they must do the same and have All Seven-Pueblo meetings, in Hopiland and send delegates from their seven villages to talk over things and know each other's troubles. Also, they are entitled to their connection with the New Mexico tribes and can send delegates to the All-Pueblo council meetings there.

I told them that a lot of outsiders would tell them not

to take this Bill, for this Bill is no good for the white people.

I told them that in past times, the Government tried to make white people out of us, and force us into different ways by schools and things, but it looks now they have turned around and are giving us back to our own Indian ways and this Bill helps us to that. But there are still people in the Indian Service who don't understand this yet, and there are some of those who are against the Bill. And I said, "I know no white man came here and told you this Bill is good, like I come to tell you, who am an Indian, myself.

"I do it because I know all our situation and our religious problem myself. I am not afraid to talk about that to you.

"I have property myself in my Pueblo and why should I come here and advise you to take this Bill if it wasn't any good? I am in the same place as you are. I would be foolish to come here and advise you to take it if it wasn't any good."

This is what I said at all the different villages and, of course, I said a lot more things.

Then, they asked me questions.

They asked me, "How could we vote without having any Governor?"

I said, "You could elect a Governor first. When the time come to vote on the Bill, you will already have a Governor."

I said, "I don't know how it will work out exactly. Maybe the Commissioner has a plan for you."

Some villages they have just one Chief. Polacca, they have three.

I visited all seven villages many times. I had several meetings in several villages. But in two villages, I couldn't get any meetings. That was Mushongovi and the one next to it. They had already heard about the Bill from one of their people named Phillip and they are in favor of it. They have a copy of the Bill and understood it, but all the men of the villages were scattered out working, and we could not get them together.

At Walapi, they were against the Bill when I got there. At the end of the meeting I had there, they said, "Before you came, we were against this Bill. Our white friends who told us about it, never explained as you have done. We didn't like this Bill but now we like it."

At Hotevilla, they just listened to me and said nothing. Then at the end of the meeting, the Chief said, "I am going to write to John Collier and ask him all about this." I said, "All right. Write carefully and make a petition and have your men sign it and John Collier will explain to you better than I do," I said.

I said, "We have got a real friend in John Collier. He really likes Indians. In past time, we had Commissioners against us who tried to stop our ceremony dances and our dances-religious. They nearly destroy us; call our ways bad or moral or something, and put in the paper they are going to stop us. But John Collier fight for us with the Indian Defense Association and he save us. Now, he look far ahead and it is like he is putting a wall all around us to protect us—and this Wheeler-Howard Bill is this wall. And no white man or grafter can come inside and take away our land or our religion which are connected together."

219

I said, "Otherwise, if we don't take this Bill, our white neighbors are all round the edge of us, they always *look*, they always look what they going to see! And maybe, they see gold. They might see coal. And if we had the allotment, the white men might begin to loan money to some Indian boy or girl because they see something on their land. And the boy or girl might want to buy an automobile and will lose their land in a few years because they have borrowed on it. That is enough to finish the Indians. You have no place to hang your hat or shawl. No house, no home. And that all be destroyed."

I told them now we're lucky because the President, Mr. Ickes and the Commissioner are all on the side of the Indians. In times to come, maybe, another kind get in and want to go back to the old treatment. But if we have come under the Wheeler-Howard Bill, they cannot get at us and we are safe from them.

I said a whole lot more things but it cannot all be written down. Anyway, they understood what I meant.

I explained to them how they would vote for the Bill just as we did here.

And I also told them how to vote for their officers for their own government.

The Bill said election on it will be coming in June and I think someone should go back in the Spring and make it fresh in their minds.

Teddy and Hanne help me a lot in understanding all about the Bill, myself. They will make a report, too.

Your friend,

Antonio Lujan.

220

"There! I guess I can talk English when I want to," said Tony when he was through.

"Flies buzzing" or not we have had some wonderful spontaneous talk in that room, though it has never been predictable or certain to come off when it was hoped for. It takes just the right amount of listening to produce really good talk, and the right kind of listeners. One wrong listener in a roomful of people where two or three are talking and the rest are audience, can inhibit an inspired flow and turn the evening trivial.

Then there are the people who aren't talkers or listeners either, who just sit. I must admit I have numbers of these whom I love, who have no words, and no interest in abstract ideas or theories, but who have their own being. These people can sit in a room and give out a vital emanation so that one feels enriched by their presence. They are alive, they feel or sense life passing through them and they deepen one's own being. But there are others who don't exist at all in their own bodies, who are merely shadows. These I do not have around, or not for long. Just as there are two kinds of places where I do not go, to places I do not like and to those who do not like me, so there are certain types of people I will not have near me, those who are insignificant in their being, and those who are trivial-minded and who neutralize other people's values.

The summer evenings are long and pleasant. If the smoke grows too thick in the room there is always the garden, sometimes with the moon falling upon the trees, turning them into great, motionless round masses with gleaming tops, black underneath, and filtering through the tightly woven roof of branches over the bandstand and shining on the black, silent water flowing underneath.

Leave the house and the voices and the music and slip out to the darkness. Part the curtain of drooping willows in front of the bandstand and fall upon one of the swings under the trees out there. Listen to the night and the lovely sounds that break its quiet. Far away in the hills the coyotes are howling and this comes down to me like plaintive Penitente singing, muted and sad; there is a faint croaking down in the orchard that comes from the rusty mocking bird that has spent so many summers there. He stirs in his sleep and gives a few lilts of his song and it seems inutterably ancient and passé in the darkness, and one's heart begins to ache for no reason—just the vague wistfulness over the imperfection of life that creeps in on one sometimes.

There is a slight rustle on the thick foliage outside this hiding place out there among the hollyhocks, thick in the flagstones, and a small sniff!

There she is, poking her dark head through the swaying

willows that hang to the ground, and seeking one out, always finding one, no matter where one goes. "Hello," I say, in a matter-of-fact voice. "Poor little Pooch."

"Yes, indeed," she seems to answer, bustling up, full of enthusiasm, showing her two tusks in a wild grin. Not apologetic like so many dogs, not curving and cringing and begging for mercy, but companionable in her sense of equality, and having a preference for certain people. She gives a vast heave up on to the swing, taking a chance of landing, and makes it, in the middle of me. She gives one smelly swipe up into my face with hers to see if I am all there, and then she crawls down to my feet and curls up with one of her contented groans. "How perfect!" she seems to sigh, "just her and me and all the others forgotten . . . !" So she goes to sleep, having somehow restored my own well-being and comfort just when I was losing it. Dogs can do that for one sometimes.

In August our house is full of the smell of preserving and pickling. Crates of peaches from Velarde down in the Rio Grande Valley stand waiting in the storeroom, and in the late evenings we go out and bring in bowls of them to eat: large, fuzzy, luscious peaches that Beatrice puts up in mason jars, a couple of dozen at a time. Max brings in the green tomatoes, the little cucumbers, cauliflowers, and the onions, and she makes all the pickles, bread-and-butter pickles, mustard pickles, piccalilli, and already she has made clear watermelon pickle from the rinds of those we had all summer.

Quinces come over from Raton for preserving; neighbors have given us some crab apples, currants and raspberries, and we have rows of glasses full of clear jellies on the shelves in the big cupboard.

Strings of garlic from the garden are hanging up from the beam and in the cellar Max has stored by now the onions, cabbages, beets and carrots.

We don't often go down to Santa Fe in the summertime, so, when we do, we see with a pang that autumn is upon us, for all the miles between here and there where we dip down into the low country, are yellow miles with the highway bordered with the bright fall flowers, long borders of sunflowers, and close-growing wild blossoms; the fields are harvest fields, pale shining wheat and corn spread out between the blue mountain ranges.

Here, where we live, the autumn has come upon us imperceptibly and we have not noticed its gradual approach. A yellowish tinge comes over the big cottonwood trees so slowly we do not see it until we go away and come back, then our eyes are freshened and we suddenly see that summer is over.

We know it then. We feel how cool the evenings are and how early the sun sets, and we would be sorry if we did not enjoy the changed feeling in the air, sorry because, like leaves falling, people will depart, the hill will be emptied of everyone but ourselves. We will be alone a great deal more by the time October is here and the heart contracts, for looking ahead it seems a lonely time is coming, but we put it out of our minds.

We watch the trees change color rapidly now, and riding to the Pueblo we snatch the wild plums off the bushes as we pass. They are warm and juicy and have a sharply sweet taste. It is nice to fill the pockets of one's riding coat and eat them as one goes.

The sunshine seems yellower, and it blazes down in a full, walloping kind of heat that is intense because of the cold edge already in the air. In the fields the Indians are harvesting their wheat and threshing it, trying to get it all in before San Gerónimo Day. After that date they will take in the corn.

In all the orchards now the fruit is falling on the ground and there is a magnificent abundance in the red and white apples. We cannot take care of so much fruit and I let the Indians come to take it away, and Max and Jose gather what they need for their families.

Little boys come asking for apples and we give them what they can carry in their sacks. The air is sweet with a fruity smell and the little pigs grow larger and run here and there all over the place, eating as fast as they can!

Our oats are cut and have been threshed and the fields are pale shining stubble, but there is a lot to eat in them yet, so Charley, Tony and Rosy are turned out to wander where they like. The first day they are loose they eat all the sweet peas that bloomed in the summer in the garden around the Pink House. Never mind! That is over.

Now Max transplants the geraniums into pots and brings them into the house for the winter. All the window sills have geraniums and begonias in them, cut way back, and soon they will start to bloom.

The trees change color quickly now for there is frost at night and they are showing every shade of yellow against the dark mountains. The distance turns a deeper blue for all the yellow near us.

The leaves shiver a little and begin to rattle on the branches. At first every year, when this dryness comes upon the beautiful trees, it seems a little ominous behind the beauty, but one grows accustomed to it.

The desert behind the house turns yellow with fall flowers, and in dry years there are big clumps of purple asters growing wild everywhere. The autumn colors here are purple and yellow and there seems to be more of an overflow of blooming and burgeoning than at any other season, like a last fling of life before the sleepy winter months.

San Gerónimo Day comes. The patron saint's day of the Indians—but it is primarily the harvest feast. The shrine at the head of the track is made of yellow branches held above their heads, so it looks at a distance like a little group of trees moving.

The Koshare climb the tall, slippery pole to win the harvest prizes fastened at the top: the corn, the pumpkins, the melons and the sheep.

There is a sound of laughter and rejoicing in all the Indian houses, the feeling of happy, autumn security is in the air.

But, before the day, down in Taos, the Plaza is a vast cloud of dust from the tourist cars. From all over they come to see the Indian Fiesta, but of late the Lions Club has advertised it as being two days ahead of the real date, hooking themselves onto San Gerónimo and offering entertainment to keep the travelers here longer for the benefit of the town, abortive races, parades, and what-not that never quite come off.

The soldiers come up from Santa Fe to take charge of the town. They are very efficient and hard-boiled and they direct the aimless travelers, sending them to right and left. There is a vague, empty search for fun going on, a continuous movement without any known goal. A Texan calls out to the Santa Fe traffic man: "You going to put on something here tomorrow?" And he replies with a large, magnanimous wave of the hand towards the Pueblo: "Naw! Tomorrow we're giving it to the Indians."

October, and all the tourists have departed. Hardly an outside license to be seen on a car!

After the trees are fully turned and are like torches of fiery yellow, often with coral red tips, and others are big round balls of radiant, sun-colored loveliness, they have a long quiet pause before the end. Day after day of Indian summer passes, breathless, when the whole valley is immobile and every leaf is motionless, shining golden and still. What days! One moves in a dream through the country, scarcely able to believe one's eyes, for the wonder of it.

On a crisp morning in October when the hills are veiled soft with smoke from burning leaves, it is delicious to ride up to the cedars and get an armful of branches covered with blueberries. We pile them in a corner of the Big Room to dry and every day Albidia will burn a piece after she has swept and dusted the rooms. The sweet wholesome fragrance penetrates every part of the house, refreshing the air, and it has a curious effect of composing the life and the nerves of everyone, and establishing a feeling of order and clarity for the whole day.

The hills are misty and blue with the autumn haze—the Sacred Mountain is intensely somber with purple depths in its canyons, and the sun moves serenely uninterrupted across the cloudless, deep blue sky.

Now the water is let to flow in the ditch for no one is irrigating any more. All the tension is gone—the wild plums cover the ground beneath the bushes, left over from what the Indians gathered for their jams and drying; the apples make a red and yellow pattern under the trees; the water seems no luxury now, running away to the Gulf of Mexico, and there is a kind of abandon and relaxation all through nature that means the end of summer.

And the thick hedges of wild brier rose are covered all over with the scarlet hips and haws of departed flowers that have passed into the sterile rose-fruit. They shine like holly berries, thicker than the bronze leaves about them, and for lack of other blossoms, one cuts branches off and takes them home for the house. But in the rooms, they lose their vivid luster and turn dim and insignificant.

The nights are cold now and the rime is on the grass in the mornings. By nine o'clock everything sparkles with the thaw, diamonded and draped in blue wisps of autumn mist. It is time to open the big chest and take out warm dresses and coats and they have to be hung on the line behind the house to get rid of the smell of camphor.

Jose goes up to Tienditas and drives the long string of black colts down. The feed is all gone up in those fields and now they are taken up to the Pueblo to eat up what is left in the fields there after the harvest.

Soon the day opens with a large white cloud soaring up over the Pueblo and a wind rises. It whirls the yellow leaves around and around against the blue sky, and they begin to run away over the ground, turning over and over.

The air is full of the rustle of dry leaves falling and blowing into drifts. They brush across one's face and one has to shut one's eyes against them. In other days there was a sharp pain at the sudden autumn ending, at the sight of the trees being stripped, the air full of the scattering leaves, but now I only know a feeling of pleasure in it, almost a feeling of peace. This is new and strange and has taken a long time to come, this feeling of complacence when the sky darkens and the air grows harsh, and all the yellow leaves blow across the sky. It is something like the Indians feel, perhaps.

Now the brown water in the ditch is full of yellow leaves floating down and the Indians like to bathe in the river on these early mornings when it is scented with them. They say it is the healthiest time of all to go in the creek.

The winds come from far now. They sweep in wide blasts across the plain and buffet against the walls. The branches of our big cottonwood tree are empty and crackle together. Only a few obstinate leaves cling to the tips. Autumn is turning into winter and there is a fire burning in every room in the house, and all the little houses on the hill are forsaken.

But remember what Thomas Bailey Aldrich wrote:

"What is more cheerful now, in the Fall of the year, than an open wood fire? Do you hear those little chirps and twitters coming out of that piece of apple wood? Those are the ghosts of the robins and bluebirds that sang upon the bough when it was in blossom last Spring. In Summer, whole flocks of them came fluttering about the fruit trees under the window: so I have singing birds all the year round."

It is easy to build fires with the little cakes of ashes mixed with kerosene oil that Ruth has taught us all to make. Stack the sticks upright, as we do here, emulating the Indian way, and thrust a cake of the gray mash under them. It is dying to burn, to catch and explode into flame. In a second, the chimney is all ablaze. Out in the Pueblo the Indian women sit together cozily in great heaps of corn, shucking the ears. They strip off the harsh husks and their sensitive fingers enjoy the pleasant contact with the ivory-hard, polished ears.

The brittle husks pile up around them and they toss the ears to one side to be woven into long strings and hung out to dry on their roof tops. Pink, yellow, light red, crimson and white—they have all the sunset colors in them. So often my friends from other places take home some colored corn to plant, always hoping it will come out in the same bright hues in their fields. But no! It comes out just like ordinary corn.

The women feel like queens, sitting with these riches surrounding them. Nothing is wasted. The discarded husks will be fed to the horses and cows later on. The Pueblo is strewn with them for they are carried about on the wind, but afterwards everything will be cleaned up when the Governor gives his order to do so from the housetop. His voice is heard in every room, in every corner of the village. People go on with their work or their conversations, but the Pueblo voice reaches them, filtered into the consciousness that is always awake and ready to hear.

The turkeys are very evident in the short stubble of the field now. They are big and black and burnished and shine like obsidian, and soon we will eat them. Turkey meat never tastes good until after the ground is cold, and old Jenny, who used to cook for us once said: "Don't you know, ma'am, that's why we have Thanksgiving in November?"

In these days the pigeons suffer more than at any other time. Huge owls swoop down at night and sit near the dovecotes waiting for a chance to alight upon a roof and surprise one of those who have to roost outside. The big hawks circle all day above them and they, too, wait for night to fall, when they will swoop down and claw a young bird from the nest. Max sets traps baited with raw meat and sometimes in the morning he finds a wide-winged fierce bird caught by a leg, fluttering and agonized.

The yellow leaves we gathered to put in the big black jars inside the house are dried and there is already a little gray dust on them. Why do lovely things last so short a time? Now we have to send to Santa Fe when we want fresh flowers, for even the chrysanthemums in the garden are finished!

Well—close all the doors and lie by the fire, and enjoy the smell of roses and carnations. Burn the osha root now to keep the air fresh. Give up to winter and the sights and sounds of its season.

Sometimes the heart tightens up, though. . . .

Now I went out to the kitchen to the telephone, but who should I call up? I had done that, once or twice, long ago, when Tony didn't come home; I had called a garage and sent a car out looking for him, and this made him so mad that I never repeated it.

"I sitting there with my friends, and a Mexican come knock at the door and ask if they seen me, and say you been sending for me! Make me feel very foolish! I not a child that you send for me!"

"But I thought maybe you had an accident and needed help!"

"I not the kind that have accidents. You know me very well—how careful."

Yes, it was true, but why couldn't I feel it? And why do I go on year in and year out, feeling frightened if he stays away late at night? Most of the other women here turn off their lights and go to sleep, whether their men are home or not. Why can't I learn to do so?

I sat down before the fire and smoked a cigarette and began to feel sorry for myself, and this took the edge off the worry. It really isn't worth it, I thought, to live here in this solitude, shut in by the winter, when everyone has gone somewhere else and is having an interesting time! But, alas! I remembered that I was here because I chose to be, and that no other kind of time anyone was having meant a thing to me, compared with my life, the way I had built it here. This was best for me, this home in the valley, where my work stretches far out ahead of me.

Yes, this was my bed I had made, and I would lie on it, and for the most part it was better than others', only the hard parts sometimes seemed harder than theirs, as I believe they are. But even in the summer, really, especially in the summers, the worst things happen, I consoled myself.

I thought of places in the village, to see if I had rather be there than alone up here. I suppose I could dress, and with some fortitude I could make my way down.

I thought of Mike's, with little tables and chairs, each with its colored cover, and the little bar at the end of the room, all shining bottles. There would be a few people in there having sandwiches and beer or highballs. It would be cheerful and cozy and not a bit noisy in Mike's place; but I hadn't the habit of it. Like always, no matter how miserable, I'd rather be home!

In some houses, people would be playing bridge, and when they were through there would be some famous Taos food brought out on the dining table. They don't make better cake anywhere in the world than they do in Taos, and the most wonderful coffee! People here know how to drink three cups of coffee at the end of an evening and then go right off to bed and sleep like tops!

I returned to my warm, serene room upstairs, and let anxiety rise in me until I was flooded with it. I ceased to oppose it, and let the trouble possess me.

Suddenly, outside my window, there was a loud, long-drawn-out howl, followed by a startling chorus of barks, rising like shrill laughter. It sounded like a hundred throats giving tongue in the still, cold night.

Coyotes down from the hill! Often we heard them in the distance, like fiends gathering as winter deepened and hunger drove them near, but rarely so close as this. The smell of fresh meat must have attracted them until they padded stealthily down through the unbroken snow to the wire-screened door of the meat-room.

Zero hour in truth, it seemed to me, now, as midnight showed on the little clock beside the bed, and I wondered if I would ever feel happy and at ease again. No matter that tomorrow the house would be full of voices, or that yesterday, only yesterday, we had had such fun with Alexandra and Spud and the others, dancing here all the evening, and doing puzzles. There was only Now, and I was unable to endure it.

Then I was driven to the center of being, as always before in hard moments, all through my life: in, in, until the point was reached that is the most living kernel of us all, and I said: "Please make him come. *Now!*" over and over, and this loosened the constraint within and lighted me up with peace. I knew beyond doubt that everything was all right, so I would not have worried any more, even if Tony hadn't come until morning.

But I didn't have long to wait after that. Far below in the house I heard the front door bang shut, and then his slow, steady step through the house, till it was mounting the stairs.

I flew through the rooms to meet him.

236

"Oh, Tony!" I cried, "I was so afraid something had happened to you. Why are you so late?"

His face looked smooth and benevolent as he put his kind hand on my shoulder.

"What can happen?" he asked, gently. "I wish you not worry like that! I had a nice time with my friends and we gambled a little: two, three dollars. I took my beans out to the Pueblo to Sofina, then she gave me coffee. Why you frightened like that?"

"Such a night—the storm—"

"Don't you know the moon is shining?" he said, smiling; and he pulled the curtain back from the window to show me.

Sure enough, it was shining, and the desert was spread out so clear and visible that I could see the shadow of the whole house, a dark reflection of itself upon the snow.

PATIO AREA OF BIG HOUSE IN WINTER

THE BIG HOUSE IN SPRING

Louis Beye '7